# DENVER'S BEST
# DIVE BARS

# DENVER'S BEST DIVE BARS

## Drinking and Diving in the Mile High City

### DREW BIXBY

**Brooklyn, New York**

Gamble Guides is an imprint of
Ig Publishing
178 Clinton Avenue
Brooklyn, NY 11205
www.igpub.com

## Denver's Best Dive Bars
## (arranged by location)

### Central Denver
Barricuda's
Barry's on Broadway
Brewery Bar II
Brown Barrel Tavern
Bulldog Bar
Charlie Brown's Bar & Grill
Cherry Cricket
Club 404
Don's Club Tavern
Gabor's
Lancer Lounge
Lion's Lair
M&M's
Nob Hill Inn
Ogden Street South
Park Tavern & Restaurant
PS Lounge
Roslyn Grill
Sancho's Broken Arrow
Satire Lounge
Skylark Lounge
Squire Lounge
William's Tavern

### Downtown
Carioca Café (Bar Bar)
El Chapultepec
Herb's
My Brother's Bar
Old Curtis Street Bar
Shelby's Bar & Grill
Star Bar
Tarantula Billiards
Wazee Supper Club

### West
Ace-Hi Tavern
Berkeley Inn
Casa Bonita
Edgewater Inn
Hill-Top Tavern
King's Court
Micky Manor
Music Bar
Rosa Mia Inn
Rustic Tavern
Squeeze Inn
The Viking
White Horse Bar

## East

The Dirty Duck Bar
Dr. Proctor's Lounge
Hangar Bar
R&R Denver
Ram Lounge
Retreat Lounge
Sam's Bar & Lounge
Thunderbird Lounge

## North

Arabian Bar
Ease On In Lounge
The Grizzly Rose
JD's Neighborhood Bar
Mr. A's Restaurant & Lounge
Phil's Place
Ron & Dan's Keg
Scoreboard Restaurant & Lounge
Sidewinder Tavern
Stockyard Saloon
Welcome Inn
Y Not Lounge

## South

BJ's Carousel
Bonnie Brae Tavern
Bushwacker's Saloon
Campus Lounge
Candlelight Tavern
Gennaro's Lounge
Kentucky Inn
Len and Bill's Lounge
Lincoln's Road House
Stadium Inn

## The Shots-No-Chasers List

Columbine Steak House & Lounge
Baron's Restaurant & Lounge
Beer Depot Lounge
The Filling Station
Lakeview Lounge
Pete's Greek Town Café
The Recovery Room
Ziggies

## Boulder

Broker Bar
Dark Horse
Outback Saloon
Rocky Flats Lounge
The Sink
Catacombs Bar
Sundown Saloon
Walrus Saloon

## I-70 Mountain Corridor

Kermitts Roadhouse
Little Bear Saloon
Morrison Inn
Red Ram Restaurant & Saloon

## Acknowledgements

I'm hardly an expert. On anything, really, but especially the city and state in which I'd lived less than five years when I began the process of researching and writing this book, a place inhabited by a people more proud than any I've ever encountered in these united states. I knew from the beginning that I couldn't let Denver down, and that felt heavy. So I asked for help, and I got it—not only in the form of advice and expertise about the city's best joints, but also rides, rounds, encouragement and companionship. To the friends and extended family of barflies listed here—and many more whom I will never forgive myself for forgetting: I couldn't have done any of this without you. Wherever you go, whatever you do in this life, may you always have a wooden nickel waiting when you arrive.

To my incredibly patient and understanding wife, Maggie, who made herself busy while I was writing and missed me terribly while I was getting shit-faced with strangers: Most women could not have endured. You did. I love you.

To Chuck, Noel, Darren, Jessica and Joe, who always answered my calls for companionship: Thanks for making the road less lonely.

To Sean, Blakey, Jesse, Erin, Neddy and everyone else who did their damndest to make sure I didn't miss anywhere. Inevitably, I still did, but I have all of you to thank for many of the places I didn't.

To everyone at *Westword*, though especially Patty and Dave, who believed in my ability to write a weekly bar column: Thanks for supporting my growth as a writer, and for always accepting my copy after deadline.

And to Marc Hughes, who readily agreed to handle photography and much of the art direction for this project in exchange for an offer I can only hope to make good on over many more years of friendship: drinks on me for life. (Please support and encourage his photography, graphic design and myriad other creative endeavors by visiting www.flickr.com/marchughes and www.behance.net/marchughes.)

## Explanations, Excuses and Apologies

Dives are disappearing. Indeed, in the 10 or so months I spent researching and writing this book, the Mozart Lounge re-imagined itself as a swanky, gay piano bar; the Satire Lounge remodeled away decades of dust and degradation; Gennaro's and the Recovery Room shuttered and reopened under new ownership; and BJ's Port—just one example of many that have gone the way of the buffalo in the last five years—closed its doors indefinitely. As of this writing (June 2009), every bar featured herein is alive and kicking; whether or not that will remain true by the time you read this, I can't say with any certainty. I know the publisher imagines this book to be a guide for your own exploits and adventures, but I'm starting to wonder if it won't end up serving a more historical purpose. So be it: Enjoy these gems while you still can; remember 'em for what they were when they're gone—cheap, no-nonsense places to celebrate and escape life, one stiff pour or ice-cold beer at a time.

## What's Included, What's Not

I made the difficult decision early on to define Denver "dives" as joints —saloons, lounges, taverns, inns, roadhouses, honky ctonks and idiosyncratic others in between—with character, no less than a decade of history and a propensity for cheap drinks and low overhead. The regular clientele of a place had just as much, if not more, to do with my definition as décor. Are the Cherry Cricket and My Brother's Bar relatively expensive now and regularly filled to the gills with yuppies and suits? Yeah. But they're road-weary old-timers with life experience and good stories, regardless of how time has changed them. Are the Grizzly Rose and Casa Bonita massive and outlandish? You bet. But they're awesomely divey in their own rights, and they make Denver a better place to be. Pubs are not included, because they need their own book; strips clubs are excluded, because they're shady and filthy—and not in a good way; and bowling-alley bars, veterans' hangouts and other niche spots that serve other purposes or aren't necessarily open to the public at all times—they didn't make the cut either, though many are wonderfully divey.

One of the harder decisions I faced relates to music venues. Ignoring the fact that most are simply too young, late-afternoon/early-evening opening times and regular cover charges (to say nothing of online ticket sales) disqualified places such as Bender's Tavern, Three Kings Tavern, the Larimer Lounge, Hi-Dive and Herman's Hideaway—even though Bender's opens at 11 a.m./has a separate room for shows, and the Hideaway was a bar for 20 years before becoming a concert destination. They're all incredible, reasonably divey spots that enrich our cityscape in innumerable ways. But, in the end, I decided they were something altogether different.

Boulder and the I-70 Mountain Corridor notwithstanding, and with a few notable exceptions (Ace-Hi, Casa Bonita, Grizzly Rose, Edgewater Inn), the bars featured in these pages all reside within Denver city limits. I'm familiar with the Poundstone Amendment and its limiting effect on Denver's borders; I also recognize that the greater metropolitan area boasts dozens—if not hundreds—more dives worthy of recognition. The absence of these suburban establishments reflects only my finite resources and not any lack of merit.

Ultimately, my criteria were subjective and the end result flawed. You can help make future editions more inclusive and representative by sending suggestions and feedback to denverdives@gmail.com, and by visiting www.denversbestdivebars.com.

## About Smoking Inside

For better or worse, Denver's dives haven't been the same since the Colorado Clean Indoor Air Act went into effect more than three years ago. As noted in these pages, a select few have dodged the law via a cigar-bar exemption, and many more have gone to great lengths to provide covered (and sometimes heated) patio spaces so patrons won't just stay home and smoke with their six packs. Others—more than you might expect—simply ignore the restriction, because this is Uh-mur-ica, goddamnit, and ain't no politician gon' tell me how to run my business. I once had a bartender hand me an ashtray and remark, matter-of-factly, "If the cops show up, you brought this from home."

My decision not to name any of these sub rosa smoke-easies has nothing to do with the fact that I smoke and everything to do with the simple truth that nobody likes a narc. I couldn't believe it when *5280*, in its February 2008 "Best Bars" feature, casually named Gabor's as a (now bygone) spot to "light up." For shame. Sorry, smokers, but you're on your own here. I trust you understand.

## Dive Bar Ratings & Symbols

All bars are rated on a scale of one to five bottles of beer, with five bottles denoting the diviest.

▮ Your mother would be proud

▮▮ Your mother would approve

▮▮▮ Your mother is comfortable in most situations

▮▮▮▮ Your mother raised you better than this

▮▮▮▮▮ Your mother might be propositioned by a meth head

All bars are also rated on a scale of one to three ironic mustaches, with three denoting the highest probability of encountering hipsters.

〰〰 Presence of hipsters is unlikely or infrequent, though anything's possible.

〰〰〰〰 Tight pants, solid V-neck tees, oversized sunglasses and references to obscure art and/or viral Internet content is expected but not guaranteed.

〰〰〰〰〰〰 Known hipster hangout: Apply Irony-Off at least one hour before arriving to repel unwanted insincerity.

Finally, cash-only dives are labeled with the word CASH, and those with 7AM, 8AM or 9AM daily opening times are identified as such.

## Denver's 10 (okay, 11) Best Dive Bars
(In Alphabetical Order)

### Ace-Hi Tavern
By far the best reason to get wrecked—and subsequently stranded—in Golden.

### Carioca Café (Bar Bar)
Just because you don't want to touch any of its surfaces doesn't mean you shouldn't puke or pass out all over 'em. At dawn. For next to nothing.

### Club 404
From the prime rib to the price of a PBR, you can trust everything about Jerry Feld's 404. Except its longevity. Now for a limited time...

### Candlelight Tavern/Kentucky Inn
Same owners, similar vibes—everything you could ask for within a safe stumble along Pearl Street.

### El Chapultepec
Nightly jazz with no cover, tasty Mexican food and the cheapest drinks in Lower Downtown.

### Hill-Top Tavern
No tabs, no credit cards, no problems – good people and good times galore.

### Rustic Tavern
Tried and true, through and through: Welcome home.

### Squeeze Inn
Four hundred square feet of cramped camaradcrie never seemed so appealing.

### Squire Lounge
A whole-body condom couldn't protect you from this cross section of Colfax characters, but cut-rate cocktails and bargain-basement beer prices will surely help with the pain.

### Thunderbird Lounge
A family friendly hangout and blue-collar barroom for all walks.

## Best Bar Crawls

### The Highland Crawl
Beer Depot Lounge > Baron's Restaurant & Lounge > Berkeley Inn

### The Downtown Crawl
Carioca Café (Bar Bar) > Old Curtis Street Bar > Star Bar > Herb's > El Chapultepec

### The East Colfax Crawl #1
Nob Hill Inn > Roslyn Grill > Sancho's Broken Arrow

### The East Colfax Crawl #2
Squire Lounge > Satire Lounge > Lion's Lair .

### The East Colfax Crawl #3
Pete's Greek Town Café > PS Lounge > Bulldog Bar

### The Capitol Hill Crawl
Gabor's > Park Tavern & Restaurant > Barricuda's

### The Capitol Hill/Governor's Park Crawl
Charlie Brown's Bar & Grill > Lancer Lounge > Don't Club Tavern

### The South Broadway Crawl
Club 404 > Barry's on Broadway > Brown Barrel Tavern > Skylark Lounge

### The Way South Broadway Crawl
Bushwacker's Saloon > Len & Bill's Lounge > Gennaro's Lounge

### The South Pearl Crawl
Candlelight Tavern > Kentucky Inn > Lincoln's Road House

### The Sheridan Boulevard Crawl
Rustic Tavern > Edgewater Inn > Lakeview Lounge

## Dive Bar Décor

If it ain't got at least half of the following, it probably ain't a dive.

Actual wooden nickels
A.M. and P.M. happy hours
Autographed/decorated dollar bills tacked to the ceiling and/or walls
Bartenders who leave the bar unattended to smoke
Bathrooms too dirty or dysfunctional to use
Boxed wine
Carpet
Cash-only policies
Chip clips
Communal sinks/mirrors located in common areas
Compact-disc or vinyl jukeboxes
Customers who pay with change
Dozing old men
Early-ass opening times
Erotic pictures for sale in the bathroom (usually next to condom dispensers)
Fly swatters and/or bug zappers
Free popcorn/peanuts/snack mix
Frozen pizza machines, Crock-Pots and microwaves
Handwritten signs on paper or cardboard (often neon-colored)
Knickknacks, bobble heads, carnival prizes or other crap behind the bar
Liquor bottles with the prices written on the labels
Mismatched stools, chairs, tables and glassware
Natural Light on tap
Payphones
Photos of regulars
Pickled anything (usually eggs) in a jar
Random games of chance
Sports memorabilia and/or NASCAR shit
Sports pools (squares)
Stained ceiling tiles
Trophies
Trough-style urinals (preferably filled with ice cubes)
Tube (or rear-projection) televisions
Vending machines containing snacks, cigarettes, and condoms
Wood paneling

**Brown Barrel**

# CENTRAL DENVER

## Barricuda's

1078 Ogden Street
Phone: 303-860-8353

I have every intention of drinking on my first trip to Barricuda's, but it doesn't happen. I glance longingly at the beer taps—Swithwicks? No. Guinness? Huh-uh—but can't talk myself into a cold one. I make eyes at a Bloody Mary two tables over and try not to spit up. My mouth tastes like two packs of cigarette butts, and my skin smells like a dripping-wet beer-pong table. I close my eyes and think hair of the dog, hair of the dog, hair of the dog, but I quickly get the spins and have to grip the table for balance, my bottle-rocket-residue-stained fingernails a painful reminder of a Fourth of July party gone horribly right. It's no use. Instead I rely on overeating—chips and guac, eggs Benedict with browns, biscuits and gravy—and six or seven Sprite refills, which do wonders for my stomach but little for my head. I go home and nap until the sun goes down.

Four days later, I return, this time for happy hour. I belly up, flip through the menu—expansive even without the breakfast pages — and drink my first two beers in silence while watching a home-run derby on television. Over the course of the next two hours, the three or four televisions within eyeshot of the bar show everything from ultimate fighting to reality drivel to the original Jaws. Star, who has taken over bartending for Josh, keeps both my beer and water full and somewhat neurotically switches between satellite-radio channels — country-Western (Merle Haggard), hits (Beyoncé), indie rock (At the Drive In)—until the bar gets busy enough for people to feed the Internet jukebox. Some guy in a blue bandanna and a Led Zeppelin hoodie plays "Sunday Bloody Sunday," so Star turns it up with her remote and we all sing along.

At some point, I switch from $2 PBRs to pitchers of Bud (always $6) and start making friends. I talk baseball with an older gentleman on the next stool who I can tell would love to take me home. More stray (straight + gay) than gay, Barricuda's is a home away for all kinds of characters. There's the guy without an ID who swears he's of age (he has a "goddamn DOC number, for chrissakes"). He speaks loudly, engaging everyone who accidentally makes eye contact, and tells us that he's getting drinking cramps. This, it turns out, is what occurs when you take lots of short gasps of air while drinking. I suggest that he drink slower, and he laughs like it's the most asinine thing he's ever heard before telling me that drinking whiskey often gives him collarbone kinks.

While smoking outside, I meet a Haight-Ashbury hippie with a gray ponytail who has just finished a joint with two others and is now looking to bum a cigarette. Mine are menthol (he's allergic), so he snorts a couple shakes of German snuff off the back of his hand before trying to sell me hallucinogens and then asking to borrow my phone. He struggles to dial ("It's the THC, man"), so I do it for him, and when he's finished he tells me that the Colombian guy he just spoke with refers to him as "muchos locos marijuana" and that he's gotta go. Peace, dude.

Back at the bar, I meet up with one of the other joint smokers. He pulls at a mixed drink (always $2.50 wells at Barricuda's) through a straw and tells me he's so stoned he doesn't know whether he's here or there. I laugh in a you-should-see-yourself-right-now kind of way and feel a little jealous. He stands, then forgets why, and figures that as long as he's standing he might as well tell a terribly inappropriate joke about showering with a nine-year-old boy. I grimace and he saunters off. Later, I watch him and three other guys make pirate noises while taking a round of shots and I think:

Goddamn, am I glad I came back.

## Barry's on Broadway

58 Broadway
Phone: 303-722-8489

Hipster Scale

Dive Bar Rating

"Oh, my gawd, I'm going to die!" exclaims the brunette seated to my left, the one with the new-haircut glow, probably from Stun! next door. It's pretty dark inside Barry's on Broadway (the former home of Skylark Lounge), but from where I'm sitting, the cut looks good—a little short in the back, but nothing to scream about. "I had to buy Newports today because they were out of Kools by work!" she continues, at which point the six or seven of us within earshot turn back to our beers and collectively roll our eyes. I'd arrived with just under an hour left of the bar's 2 to 6 p.m. happy hour, but $1 off everything doesn't strike me as all that happy, so I opted for the Wednesday special—$2.50 import bottles—and am drinking Coronas.

The jukebox, at least for the moment, lies dormant, and the two large, corner-mounted televisions blare white fuzz. The place is essentially asleep. I take it as a cue to play the Megatouch machine to my right, choosing the Jumble Crossword game and unscrambling words for a good twenty or thirty minutes on the ten credits that are already loaded. During my solitary word-nerd stupor, I don't even notice that my beer is low, but bartendress Becka does. "Hey, Andrew, you want another?" she hollers while bending over the bottle fridge. I'm startled at first—Andrew? Only my mother calls me that—until I realize she's the kind of 'tender who remembers the names on credit cards. I holler back: "Yes. Please."

A quick piss and five-minute smoke later, I re-enter the front door to find the place drastically transformed. The juke is now blaring everything from terribly mainstream country to mind-numbing techno, and there's a near-shirtless, Kid Rock-looking guy in a baseball cap dancing all over the open aisle—stumbling through a very broken line dance one moment, falling into the bathroom and making gagging sounds the next. Becka and I make eyes that say, "Glad we're not that guy." And herein lies the primary value of Barry's: On this stretch of if-only-this-was-Portland-or-Brooklyn-or-Berkeley South Broadway, it's all about being seen—in the hipster bars, boutiques, book stores and various other spaces selling second-hand wares. But not here. Here you find cheap-enough drinks slung in low light by good people. You find microwaved cheeseburgers and frozen pizza for pennies on the dollar. You find the usual entertainment (billiards and video games) if that's what you're looking for, but a quick look around usually provides all the entertainment you need.

## Double Up Poker Machines

**Arabian Bar**

**Rosa Mia Inn**

**Sidewinder**

**Old Curtis Street Bar**

**Campus Lounge**

# Brewery Bar II

150 Kalamath Street
Phone: 303-893-0971

*Hipster Scale*

*Dive Bar Rating*

Born in 1954 in the now-defunct Tivoli Brewery, the original Brewery Bar was a simple neighborhood joint forced to vacate and relocate 20 years later to make way for the development of the Auraria Higher Education Center (which opened in 1977 and still uses the Tivoli as its student union). Thus Brewery Bar II was born on Kalamath Street, where it continues to delight a surprisingly Anglo clientele 35 years later.

First, the food: It's pretty good. It's better than decent. It's growing on me, but I certainly don't shit my pants with excitement when my Styrofoam plate emerges from the kitchen and the first forkful hits my tongue. Yet every Best Of season, the local media can't string together enough compound adjectives to describe how incredibly hot and delicious the green chile is; they send plaques and posters to commemorate their decisions, and BB II hangs 'em up with the rest of the crap (including but not limited to: a computer printout reading, "Welcome to the BB II where there's No Gas Shortage here! Fill 'er Up!"; hockey photos and the gamut of Broncos memorabilia; and another sign: "Children left unattended will be towed at owner's expense.")

The entire space is technically two rooms, though it feels more like one incredibly long corridor with tables and chairs set up for a potluck. The walls and carpet are maroon with touches of wood for good measure, and though the ceiling tiles have clearly been replaced since the smoking ban, they still appear worse for the wear. Toss in some tacky, white track lighting (why so bright, BB II?) and an open-window kitchen with a soda fountain in full reach of the nearest table, and you're here.

But if you're not drinking a Tiny—24 ounces of beer or margarita at bargain prices—then you might as well not be. More than 30 types of tequila is fun, but beware the margarita mix: it's not for everyone. Every week, a different tequila's on special for $3.00, and the standard 3-6 p.m. happy hour extends until 9 p.m. on Mondays.

Which brings me to the real bummer about Brewery Bar II: With early-ass closing times, you'll never see 10 p.m. from the inside. Take the green chile challenge (current record: 13 bowls in one sitting) or drink too many Tinys, though, and you just might awake in the parking lot well after midnight.

# Brown Barrel Tavern

*76 South Broadway   7AM CASH*
*Phone: 303-777-9898*

*Hipster Scale*

*Dive Bar Rating*

Hiding in plain sight of South Broadway's trendiest, most hipster-friendly galleries, boutiques and bars, the Brown Barrel—with its unassuming, yellow "Tavern" sign and spectacular barrel-shaped entranceway—has, since the '70s (since it moved south from 3rd and Broadway), offered those in the know a simple, window-less respite from the cacophony all around it. Ignoring the entrance and a nautical theme highlighted by backlit mermaid stained glass and enough blowfish, pirate, lobster, shark and fish ornamentation to make a drunken sailor cry, the long, technically two-room bar is rather unremarkable. Though I'm sure the hundreds upon hundreds of smiling faces cut out and forever honored in 12 bronze-framed picture collages would disagree. I know Dawn, who chomps on bubble gum, reheats coffee in the microwave and paces up and down behind the bar like it's a hospital waiting room, would. But unremarkable—within the context of the Brown Barrel and South Broadway, at least—is a good thing. $2 mugs of Busch, a little entertainment (Simpsons pinball and Golden Tee machines in the back room/kitchen) and Hot Mama pickled eggs—what more could you want?

Something on the jukebox besides rock ballads and Jock Jam compilations might be nice, but five plays for a buck is pretty goddamn sweet, even if Meat Loaf's "I'd Do Anything for Love" won't play without skipping. And while the silence when the juke's asleep (no stereo otherwise) can seem a tad unnerving at first, and the ice cubes in place of urinal cakes in the pissers makes for a slightly smelly bathroom experience, the irony happening in all directions outside is enough to keep me here, where the beer's cold, the cocktails cheap and the company unremarkably remarkable.

# Bulldog Bar

*3602 East Colfax Avenue 7AM*     Hipster Scale         Dive Bar Rating
*Phone: 303-333-4345*

My buddy Darren will never be featured on a televised episode of American Idol—not because he's a lousy singer, but because he's not lousy enough. Granted, he won't be charting on Billboard or CMJ anytime soon, either, but that doesn't say shit about his ability to nail Bowie's "Space Oddity" as a karaoke duet with his girlfriend. Mid- "Ground control to Major Tom..." one night last year, however, the bartender at Bulldog Bar began frantically ringing a large bell to signal his aversion to the current rendition. Darren had been gonged. The song went on, but the damage was done.

Earlier in the evening, when we thought we'd wandered into an irony-free karaoke night at the type of bar with a Sharpie-scribbled "One Drink Minimum" sign and a color-coded pricing system, the kind of bar that serves $3 Jäger shots and $5.75 frozen sausage pizzas all day, every day—the sort of bar where toothless townies with grease-stained hands, seasoned regulars in their Saturday-night, stretched-out-T-shirt best, and bearded, bespectacled hipsters all coalesce—we watched the fanny-pack-wearing emcee drink straight from a pitcher, fumble with the dials, and laugh as a friend of his humped and air-thrusted the stage railing while squealing high-pitched lines about fucking girls in the parking lot and the bathroom of the Bulldog.

Yet Darren got the gong? Conceptually, Gong Show karaoke is fabulously hilarious. But without full disclosure and fair warning, we all felt kicked in the neck. Others must have felt similarly, because this particular take on karaoke disappeared not long after. Still, it provides a window into the atmosphere and attitudes waiting inside the front door.

Formerly both the Monroe Tavern and the Alamo, the Bulldog sports a sizable potbellied stove by the front door for icy nights; an inviting, half-moon-shaped bar; a back room with a couple of pool tables; and a front patio for smoking with drinks in hand. Pitchers and buckets and mixed drinks and...hell, it's all cheap. Grab a seat somewhere and get drunk.

Just feel lucky you never got gonged.

# Charlie Brown's Bar & Grill

*980 Grant Street*
Phone: 303-860-1655

*Hipster Scale*
🍺🍺🍺🍺🍺

*Dive Bar Rating*
🍾🍾

I'm pretty well sauced by the time Sean and I get to Charlie Brown's. The eighty-odd-year-old bar tucked into the Colburn Hotel & Apartments—a famed '40s hangout of Beat hipsters Neal Cassady, Jack Kerouac and Allen Ginsberg—is packed, but we have no trouble finding a table on the wraparound patio (covered and heated in the winter for smokers) and an attentive waiter to bring us two bottles of MGD. I'm miffed by the lack of draft beer, as I always am when I find myself in a bar that only serves bottles, but I'm drunk already, so any beer will do.

We're here to meet Maris the Great (Google that shit. Immediately), the gay zombie who photographs himself "killing" and ass-raping hardcore bands for his cult-followed website. We scan the bar looking for Denver hardcore's favorite undead homo—we even keep an ear out for screams of pain and agony—but find no signs of him, so we drink half of our beers and then ask the waiter if he's seen a zombie walking around. "You mean the GWAR-looking dude with pink fingernails?" That's him. "I think he just left."

Shit.

We run from the patio like teenagers on a two-minute Toys 'R Us shopping spree, spreading out to cover the lobby, the parking lot and parts of the bar we might have missed the first time, then finally find him by the signature piano, singing "Joy to the World," by Three Dog Night, and growling at onlookers.

For most of the hour-plus we spend with Maris, he doesn't break character—not even when he has to remove one of his ghoulish gloves to get his credit card from under his black cape, a move I find especially hilarious. He spends most of the time staring at me while licking his teeth; when we eventually part ways (the full story is for another time), he licks both our hands and promises to see us again.

Suffice it to say that every night at Charlie Brown's isn't so un-settling, though you never know with this after-work neighborhood staple. Though it's much more than just a dark, musty piano bar, if you can catch ancient, almost-blind Paulie (last found playing one-hour sets on Tuesday nights) behind the piano, your heart better be still, your voice raised in joyful chorus. Given the size of the main room and patio, it's entirely possible to avoid the keys altogether if you so choose. Not to be missed, however, are the summer pig roasts and free bar tab (up to $30) on your birthday.

## Worst Bathrooms

### Arabian Bar

### Carioca Café (Bar Bar)

### Hill-Top Tavern

### Lakeview Lounge

### Len & Bill's Lounge

### Lion's Lair

### Ram Lounge

### Sancho's Broken Arrow

### Squire Lounge

### White Horse Bar

# The Cherry Cricket

*2641 East Second Avenue*
*Phone: 303-322-7666*

Hipster Scale

Dive Bar Rating

The Cherry Cricket—formerly Duffy's Cherry Cricket and, before that, Mary Zimmerman's Bar—didn't always have a door guy checking IDs and stamping hands at 5:30 p.m., or a forty-minute wait for a table on a Tuesday night, or a national reputation for serving more than sixty beers and some of D-Town's best burgers. It didn't always have such a cheeky, playfully impertinent marketing campaign emphasizing not only its location ("The black sheep of Cherry Creek" and "If Cherry Creek North is the diamond, we're the flaw"), but also its menu ("fancy bottled beer" and "horzidurvees" are two apt headings). It didn't always have three separate dining rooms and a fenced-in back patio, attract droves of new parents stowing fold-down strollers underneath tiny tables, inspire hundreds upon hundreds of reviews on local amateur-critic websites.

But things change. Original owners retire, sell and die. Well-intentioned bar/restaurant empires step in with remodeling money and operational manuals. Frou-frou boutiques, spas and restaurants sprout up and around like fragrant-yet-pesky wildflowers, and parking suddenly requires a credit card or coins. Life goes on.

Luckily, some things don't change. So when I visit the Cricket, I make a point to notice traces of the dive that once was—from floor (green carpet) to wall (concrete and wood paneling) to ceiling (a massive wooden centerpiece painted like a hockey rink that used to hang over the bar when it was still in the middle of the main room). Beerphernalia—much of it vintage, such as the "Have YOU Tried a Yellow Hammer?" Coors sign by the Elvis pinball machine and the Hall of Fame beer-tap case—is still scattered about; brown plastic air purifiers (holdovers from the glory, ahem, smoking-indoors days) still cover every fan frame; and the new coat of blue paint in the bathrooms? It's smeared over the trim and ceiling tiles, just as it would be in any working-stiff saloon.

The clientele, while a bit more upper-crusty than the garbage-truck drivers and swing-shifters who populated this place decades ago, is still a healthy mix of winos, women and weirdos. When I visit with my fifty-year-old mother, she's by no means the oldest hen in the coop. After fighting tooth and elbow for two stools at the bar, we lean for a good four hours, drinking pints of Wynkoop B3K and tall Colorado Bulldogs for $4 apiece, chatting with the bartenders and people watching.

My buzz shifts into fifth around 10 p.m., so I order a burger and frings and pass the time making strangers uncomfortable as I hover near their table and stare at the tri-panel fish tank separating the dining room from the kitchen. I order more drinks from Heidi (she calls me "sweetheart" with every serve) We smoke outside near the bike rack and watch through bleary eyes as the Cricket's neon sign turns an endless circle and luxury SUVs crawl by.

Things change. But for the Cricket, life goes on.

# Club 404

404 Broadway  8AM
Phone: 303-778-9605

*Hipster Scale*

*Dive Bar Rating*

To take a piss at the 404, you have to walk, essentially, through the kitchen—past the meat slicer, stacked potatoes, uncovered soups, metal racks stacked with plastic trays of baked goods and condiments needing refilling, silverware rolling. Then you pass the single sink with no mirror. Oh, and sometimes you must climb over a huge cardboard box of clear vegetable frying oil. Once inside and comfortably leaning against your forearm (or head), you listen to whatever the kitchen staff is blaring, often commercials—"Listen carefully as I explain how you can benefit from the Transforming Debt Into Wealth plan..." Back in the dingy clubhouse dining room, the green carpet is faded beyond floral-print recognition, the heater hanging from the ceiling is held together with duct tape, the patchwork of wooden squares toward the ceiling—think wooden scaffolding or kindergarten cubbies—hides decades of dirt and godonlyknowswhatelse and the ATM is out of service. Fucking great.

Since 1951, Jerry Feld and family have been welcoming Denver's dignitaries, Democrats, drug addicts and denizens from all walks of life to come in and have a drink or ten. From one flavor of vodka to 30, a modest menu to a monster offering $3 onion-ring baskets, $9 shrimp cocktail and an $18 rib eye, the 404 has seen a few changes—most notably in the remodeling of the side dining room and the addition of a spacious outdoor patio—but grows only more charming for the decades of wear.

Bearing witness to this great history are five decades of Colorado license plates hanging behind the bar; framed cards reading, "Support a union bar / First 2 drinks for the price of 1 compliments of the owner"—as well as five-panel marbled mirrors—at every booth; and hard-to-explain, retro "Bally Palm Springs" and "Bally Miami Beach" light-up number-game displays. At some point, for your comfort, Jerry installed a Filt-Air Purifier, though it's obviously obsolete now. And the compact-disc jukebox? It's inexplicably covered in red padded vinyl.

For all its yesteryear glory, however, Club 404 is in trouble. Closing time's been creeping before the midnight mark on weeknights, no thanks to a crumbling economy and a once-loyal hipster set that can barely afford a dirty 30 of PBR, let alone a bar tab. Plus, developers are lurking, promising collaborative development schemes in exchange for Jerry's signature on the dotted line. But any asshole with a carpet sample stapled to his face could tell you that condos and Club 404 could never coexist. Not for a second without the Feld family.

# Don's Club Tavern

*723 East 6th Avenue*
*No Phone*

Hipster Scale

Dive Bar Rating

Plenty of dives have personality disorders: Candlelight Tavern, Carioca Café, Squire Lounge—they all balance a blue-collar, transient daytime persona with a radically different nighttime (and weekend) identity, one dominated by hipsters, punks, college kids and the like. Chalk it up to proximity/convenience, wallet-friendly prices, a predilection for jukebox control and character, whatever. For most of its 60-year career as one of Denver's best no-bullshit bars, Don's— primarily known as Don's Mixed Drinks because of its iconic neon sign—didn't have to deal with this disorder. It was as authentic and comfortably worn out as a pair of original Chuck Taylors. But then Don died, and local conglomerate Little Pub Company stepped in. Which, let me stress, was a good thing, because as any Denverite will tell you, any Don's is better than no Don's.

But Don's has changed. The daytime, for you purists, is still relatively safe, because most of the kids are in class or their cubicles. But the 7 a.m. open time is long gone—traded for 2 p.m. on weekdays and 11 a.m. on weekends. Before you know it, the sun is setting and the meat-market-shit-show has begun. A friendly warning: After 8 p.m on a Thursday, Friday, or Saturday, the crowd of popped collars, fauxhawks and hot pants is so dense that it's difficult to find a place to stand, let alone get a drink. The simple back patio—with its space heater in winter and graffiti-covered picnic tables—is about the only tolerable place to be if you just want to get drunk (and not laid). Inside, the digital jukebox pumps hot, of-the-moment jams (MGMT at a dive? Really?) as often as it does classic rock or oldies. The whole scene is a hot, hot mess.

Speaking of the table graffiti: One notable scribble reads, "Hold your pee the bathrooms are gross." Not anymore. A recent, plumbing-failure-inspired, remodel wiped away the decades of filth and replaced it with shimmer and shine. As of this writing, another, considerably more substantial, expansion and remodel project is under way. So, while you can still play pool and mini bump shuffleboard; occasionally find Doc Wilson and his array of prosthetic legs behind the bar; and count on $2 PBRs and $3 well drinks—that is, you can still count on Don's to be a dive—you can't count on things to say the same forever.

## Gabor's

*1223 East 13th Avenue*
*Phone: 303-832-3108*

*Hipster Scale*

*Dive Bar Rating*

In the interests of avoiding a highly subjective, semantic discussion about who, exactly, qualifies as a hipster ten years into the 21st century, let me simply say that if your definition of a hipster is anyone youngish, artistic/creative and socially liberal, then Gabor's is definitely a hipster bar. If your definition is much more nuanced and involves the ironic appropriation of culture, music and fashion, then Gabor's might not be a hipster bar. Regardless: Its core clientele, unlike almost every other bar in this book, is not predominantly working class with a splash of young and fun thrown in. If anything, it's the opposite—patrons have always struck me as cool in one way or another.

This would explain the compact disc jukebox—known in every corner of Capital Hill as one of the area's finest—and the way it so successfully rides the line between juke-joint classics from decades past and both modern and contemporary indie favorites. For example: Etta James, the New Pornographers, Led Zeppelin, the Get Up Kids, Bob Dylan, Gogol Bordello, the Ramones and the Pixies—all find (or have found) a home inside this almost-always-full-of-credits box. Cool.

Retro, dim and a wee bit musty, Gabor's is decorated like a museum of studio-era Hollywood films—faux-marble Formica on the bar; red vinyl booths; black-and-white checkered floors; framed glossies of Marilyn, Gable, Garland, Wayne, Hepburn and Hayworth; fake plants and mirrors; and a touch of stained glass. Until only recently—and I mean very recently, not 2006 smoking-ban recently—the air was blue and gray and thick with mystery. Which was cool, because once the kitchen was done serving up some seriously appetizing dishes from its film-themed menu, business remained steady—proof that low-key nonsmokers and pack-a-day creatives can, in fact, coexist under private autonomy.

The energy, in general, is subdued—loners, couples and laid-back groups of friends sucking down cocktails and pints over conversation. And while the pool-table action in the back game room is often a touch rowdier, Gabor's never loses its cool.

# Lion's Lair

*2022 East Colfax Avenue*
*Phone: 303-320-9200*

*Hipster Scale*

*Dive Bar Rating*

An itty-bitty armpit of a Colfax dive—black walls; cold, concrete bathrooms; crusty everything—the Lion's Lair is worthy not just as a daytime cave for escapism and the bottle's warm embrace, but more so as a nightly variety show of Denver's best indie/punk/underground musicians and organizations. With nary enough seats around the horseshoe-shaped bar for your ska band or bike-messenger gang, expect to cram-stand and cringe as your ear drums bleed when something's poppin' on the sunken stage.

If Captured by Robots were a gutter-drunk joint, it'd be the Lair. It'd serve you Old Style and PBR from the tap with mechanical efficiency. It'd point without speaking at the giant drink-list chalkboard if you wondered about specials or availability. It'd run out of Jack or your favorite $2 can of swill, apologize disinterestedly and implore you to fucking pick something else already. It's doesn't fuck around, buddy. Deal.

Definitely stay a while: Laugh at how 90s Helen Hunt and Bill Paxton look on the Twister pinball machine tucked against the sound booth. Squint to read the hundreds of campy stickers – "I (heart) Mormon Pussy," "My kid sells dope to your honor student at Get High School"— covering the rails and beer coolers and walls. Scratch your head at the oh-so-out-of-place flatscreen TV above the door. Consider stealing some of the framed lion-themed art. But don't. Unless you want to taste Colfax concrete courtesy of the bartender.

# Lancer Lounge

*233 East 7th Avenue*
*Phone: 303-722-6484*

*Hipster Scale*

*Dive Bar Rating*

"Rita, I'm sick of this shit," Tom says of his Beck's bottle, then orders a Smirnoff screwdriver. His friends and acquaintances smirk at the switch. "This guy ain't fucking around," Rex exclaims.

"You know," Tom responds with mock irritation, "I've spent so much time learning how to drink, I oughta be able to do what I want."

"Yeah," a friend with a long white mustache snorts, "you've got a degree in drunk."

"An advanced degree!" adds Ted.

"Eh. I'm still working on my master's," Tom retorts, ending the discussion.

But I'm not so sure. Judging from the indents they leave in the green vinyl chairs when they step out to smoke and the way patrons and staff alike regard them as semi-permanent fixtures, I'd guess each of these regulars has an honorary doctorate from the Lancer Lounge. The dean, at least on this particular Sunday afternoon, is Rita, no question. Whether for high marks or heavy pours, students worship her unceasingly.

"We love you so much, Rita," an exuberantly intoxicated gay couple repeats eight or nine times in a span of two minutes.

"You're the best-looking redhead I've seen all day," a stocky fellow ordering an AmberBock pitcher admits.

"Love your nails," a woman in a hooded sweatshirt remarks, clasping Rita's left hand between both of hers for emphasis. Rita is flattered but not quite amused; she strikes me as a seasoned warhorse of a bartendress: friendly, gracious, but completely intolerant of bullshit.

Kind of like the Lancer in general. The wood paneling, low ceilings, cigarette machine, softball trophies, framed prints, football pools, bags of chips, random books, turn-page juke, Formica tables, sagging booths, even the Lord of the Rings pinball machine—it all says "Get your ass in here, but don't make me throw your ass out." The two modest-sized flatscreen TVs behind the pine bar are just about the only accoutrements that don't scream backwoods Wisconsin lodge or 1970s basement, but even these are compensated for by the thirteen-inch relic in the back showing soundless episodes of "COPS."

"Lancer Lounge: Where Friends Meet" T-shirts sell for $16 each and speak the simple truth. On the front patio, a dozen-plus people hoard every chair and share pitchers while carrying on at volumes almost loud enough to drown out the football game showing on the TVs inside. Down the bar from me, a young woman with a rusty-blond ponytail recounts for a captive audience how she lucked upon some kids in the alley smoking "the mar-uh-ju-wana" and, after helping herself, invited them to join her here. Tom offers his fellow scholars and me a round on him. And even though posted signs declare No Panic Bar (one complete hour of free well, wine and draft on Wednesday nights) Until After the Holidays, three separate happy hours each day are sure to keep the good times going. Graduation depends on it.

## Games of Chance

**Squeeze Inn**

**Kentucky Inn**

**Candlelight Tavern**

**Sidewinder**

**R&R Denver**

# M&M's

2621 ½ Welton Street
Phone: 303-295-0424

Hipster Scale

Dive Bar Rating

M&M's ain't the sort of place you'd just wander into for a drink. Not that it's hidden from street view or entirely without signage—a small, circular Budweiser sign juts out above the door, though even that's easy to miss—but these days, almost nobody wanders anywhere near Welton Street in Five Points looking for a drink unless they're also looking for live music (at Cervantes') or a deejay (at Pure Nightlife, formerly the Roxy).

Were you to happen upon M&M's (or seek it out intentionally), you'd first need to climb a steep case of wooden stairs starting at the street, turn left past the locked men's bathroom and proceed through a white door with no window. Your entire ascent would be broadcast on closed-circuit television inside thanks to an eye in the sky at the peak of your climb. Once inside, you'd find a close-knit and loyal group of predominantly black regulars, if you found anyone besides Thurman or Georgia behind the bar.

Before I ever visited, I'd heard stories. The best involved two white friends who shot their whiskey "all wrong," according to Francis, a former bartendress. As punishment, they received follow-up shots on the house—which they also shot incorrectly. So on and so forth and so many free shots later that one of the friends put his face on the Formica (and has trouble to this day recalling the night's events), they cracked the code: tap, shoot, tap, turn upside down.

Tonight, when one such friend and I trek up Mount M&M's around 10 p.m. and into the cramped quarters of the main room, we find Thurman already packing the contents of the cash register into a zipper bag bound for the bank. He eventually turns around and reluctantly serves us $2 Bud bottles, though it's obvious he was hoping to go home. But we tip well—excessively, really—so he serves us another, and another, and then an overflowing one-ounce shot of our choice on the house.

Tap, shoot, tap, turn upside down. Wait. Relax.

Thurman serves us one final Bud, throwing in a complimentary seven-ounce Bud pony for our female friend, until it's well after 11 p.m. and he mumbles something about closing time. At which point he helps Sam, the only other customer with us this whole time, down the stairs, arm-in-arm. We watch the slow descent on the tiny black-and-white tube in the corner. "You're a good friend, Thurman," I tell him upon his return. "Sam'd do the same for me," is his response.

Though this space has only been M&M's for the last five years, it began as the Porters and Waiters Club in 1936, catering to railroad and hotel employees from around the nation. As a young man, circa 1958, Thurman came in for cocktails and conversation. If the Fire Marshall has been up here in the past five years—or ever—I doubt he would hang a sign declaring occupancy code any higher than 25 or 30. Dollar bills, personalized for prosperity with pen and marker, hang by the dozens on the wall behind the liquor bottles, some so old the price-per-drink is still scrawled on the label (photocopied price lists have been posted for over a year). Pork rinds hang from metal clips on a rack beneath the sole television, which shows syndicated reruns of "The Wayans Bros." A sign dangling from the ceiling tiles reads: "Men are on this planet because vibrators can't buy drinks."

In the minutes before Thurman escorts us down the stairs and locks up behind us, he dances by himself in the small side room—first to an R&B number popular in the '90s that I can't place, then to a Little Milton track I've never heard. With the lights off and his eyes closed, Thurman's balance isn't much better than Sam's was a few minutes ago. Still, he manages to steer clear of the jukebox and the handful of padded booths while shuffling and sliding in a lop-sided circle. It don't matter.

It's not like anyone's going to just wander in.

**NOTE:** While two totally separate establishments, Roslyn Grill and Nob Hill Inn nonetheless comprise a flaming binary star of degeneracy around which many of Denver's down-and-out orbit.

An actual Craigslist Missed Connection from 2009-01-14, 4:35PM MST, titled "roslyn grill—28 (colfax)":

*ME: sitting at the window table at Roslyn blonde hair, blue eyes and big tits!!!*

*YOU: black cracked out missing most of your teeth, you may have had several std's. We met eyes and i think i might of felt something i know you did at least it looked like you grabbed your cock!! so if you read this and are interested i would love to grab a drink or crack rock!! hope to hear from you soon. yours truly La Roslyn.*

So there's that. There's also a piece of lined paper twine-tied to the stoplight just out front that reads, "Eggs, Grits, Bacon, OJ" (???). There's a kid with a skateboard who hits me up for a buck and a smoke while muttering, "Some bitch just stole $10 from me." There's a woman I see through the front windows who drops her pocketbook and doesn't notice; I scurry out, pick it up and give it to her; when I return, four haggardly dudes—shady opportunists, all of 'em—give me shit for doing the right thing; they eventually call me a good guy but don't mean it.

There's no easy way to say this, so I'm just going to: Roslyn Grill is a fucking halfway house with a full-service bar and a breakfast-all-day menu. It attracts a mostly male, hard-luck crowd banging down the door at sunrise and paying with pennies come sunset. For the past 20 years, the Roslyn—spacious, red, with a massive golf-framed mirror behind the bar and oddly feng shui glass bricks leading to the bathrooms—has been located in the middle of East Colfax's meanest stretch (if not on its meanest corner); before that, it was downtown where the Colorado Convention Center currently stands. Across the street is Denver's most beautiful church (Immaculate Conception) and only two-story McDonald's (where the bathrooms are locked and on a timer). People who love movies that don't end well "because they're more realistic" would adore the shit show that bounces back and forth between here and the Nob Hill Inn. It's so urban, so gritty, ya know?

Because they're less than a block apart and both cheap as hell, the Roslyn and Nob Hill attract the same crowd at different times—when one happy hour ends, the circus travels; if one crew has beef with another, it's posse out. If the Roslyn is the loud, large, windowed workout room at the YMCA, Nob Hill is the locker room—private (no view from the outside) and quiet (a horseshoe-shaped bar, a few booths, some terrible art and a five-plays-for-a-buck Hyperbeam Laser Disc jukebox is the whole deal). In a hilarious attempt to keep out the riff-raff and enforce its zero-tolerance policy against slinging rock, selling stolen goods, or possessing "firearms, knives, brass knuckles, etc ," the Nob, which recently celebrated its 50th birthday, pumps classical music from a speaker just outside the front door. This doesn't keep a dude in a Mizzou long sleeve and Harley cap from trying to sell me hot PS2 games. It doesn't keep a Haight-Ashbury expat two stools down from screaming about how District 6 cops are "fucking fucks," and about how once he organizes the Native Americans and the bikers, "it's kill time, man." And it doesn't keep over-anxious Danny from unwrapping a pair of ladies' Isotoners to reveal his shank. "Can't trust nobody, man," he tells me. Then: "Y'all in here the night before last? Bitch was taking off her top. It was unreal."

My sentiments exactly.

# Ogden Street South

*103 South Ogden Street*
*Phone: 303-722-0592*

Hipster Scale   Dive Bar Rating

The O. is a characteristically Wash Park neighborhood dive packed with college students shrieking and squealing their way through song after shrilling karaoke song. It's dudes with sprawling, curly side-burns and stretched-out T-shirts missing every note and lyrical cue of "Sweet Child O' Mine," yet still receiving wild applause and whooping from all corners of the bar. It's a twenty-man, ugly-Christmas-sweater stag party stumbling around acting creative and clever in greasy wigs, tweed pants and nubby turtlenecks. It's being in the way of a server or busboy no matter where you stand, and getting kicked, bumped, shouldered and stepped on by wobbling, tottering drunks and hand-holding trains of girls so glazed that only the metaphorical locomotive has any control of their bodies.

But it's Saturday night, and if you don't show up before dusk on weekends (karaoke on Friday and Saturday) to get a table and gratu-itously tip a server to remember you, don't bother. If you don't drink beer out of the bottle, expect plastic keg cups. If you don't mind your manners, you'll be tossed by a pair of tanker-sized biceps or an off-duty cop with something to prove.

Visit any other time (especially on Mondays, when it's happy hour all night), however, and you'll find Ogden Street to be a cozy joint tucked away from the chaos offering American-style appetiz-ers and sandwiches, worth-the-price pizza and a decent range of Greek specialties (the kitchen closes at 10 p.m. every night; if you live close enough, you can have the grub delivered). Come alone and snag a tattered paperback from the shelf by the bathrooms or ogle the mind-blowing flatscreen TV spread; bring a friend and play foosball or pool. The joke's on you if you're not on the expansive front patios (one is smoker friendly; the other is not) during warmer months.

But you'll really feel like the butt if you bother with Saturday nights.

# PS Lounge

*3416 Colfax Avenue*
Phone: 303-320-1200

*Hipster Scale*

*Dive Bar Rating*

Adored by denizens in every corner of our fair city's unending sprawl —revered especially by the rental junkies in the Capitol Hill/Cheesman/Congress Park hoods—the PS Lounge is a gem that shines in spite of its flaws. If the road to dive-bar royalty was, in fact, paved with good intentions, the PS would lord over all others simply because everyone through the door receives a free shot of Alabama Slammer (SoCo, OJ and sloe gin) and all ladies are handed a fresh rose courtesy of Pete, the owner. Make the mistake of expecting both on every visit, however, and risk setting yourself up for misdirected disappointment. If you receive these wonderful gifts, be thankful; if you don't, move on.

A narrow, two-room space with well-worn booths great for groups, the side billiards room features a crucial service window and shares a wall with Enzo's End, an excellent pizza joint that will deliver pies to your table. Be prepared with cash (no tabs, no ATM) and an extra fiver so you can run the compact-disc juke (everything from Cheap Trick to Johnny Cash to Three Dog night) for a jaw-dropping 25 songs. Practice patience when the CDs skip or simply don't play.

If you're going outside for some fresh air or a smoke, ditch your half-full drink behind the quaint curtains hanging from the front windows. On your way back in, heed the "Be 21 or Be Gone" sign. Notice the dust-covered trophies, the American flags, the football helmets mounted like deer heads on mahogany plaques, the playbills of Humphrey Bogart shooting pool and Cary Grant driving a convertible, the faded photos of regulars, the posters of ABBA and Elvis, Jim Morrison and Marilyn Monroe.

Settle in and settle down: If you mind your manners, Pete will treat you like long-lost family; if you don't, he'll toss you out with the wilted roses.

CENTRAL

DENVER'S BEST DIVE BARS

# Park Tavern & Restaurant

*921 East 11th Avenue*
Phone: *303-832-7667*

*Hipster Scale*

*Dive Bar Rating*

Bar time at the Park Tavern is roughly fifteen minutes fast, which means, of course, that last-call and you-can't-stay-here cries leave the mouths of bar staff between 1:30 and 1:45 (real time) each morning, sometimes earlier. Boo, hiss and other profanities. It also means that when my watch reads 4:15 p.m., my fourth Bud draft is accompanied by a red token signifying my next drink is on the house. Hip, hip and hooray! With three weekly two-for-one happy hours—9-11 a.m. Monday through Friday; 4:30-6:30 p.m. and 9 p.m.-midnight Wednesday through Monday—cashing in these colored tokens might seem simpler than fastening Velcro. But unless everyone in the group is on exactly the same consumption schedule, someone's bound to leave with one or more left over. Plus, the tokens change colors every few months, with expired colors only having value on the first Monday of every month thereafter. My friend Cole thinks they should distribute pocket-sized laminates containing all the rules; I think it's only safe to take these suckers home if the plan is to return. Soon.

The Park Tav is a plain-and-simple sports bar with well vodka on the gun ('the fuck?') a massive menu (breakfast is served every day from 8 a.m. to 4 p.m. and 10 p.m. to 1 a.m.) and plenty of tables and booths with favorable views of the flatscreen TVs. During sporting events and on weekend nights, the place is packed with a college and popped-collar crowd; it's also quite loud, whether from the turn-page jukebox or competitive screams and shrieks. Otherwise—and lately, in general, according to grumbling bartenders—things are slow and subdued.

It is by no means a dump, though it occasionally smells of harsh cleaners and fryer grease and boasts a number of divey characteristics —trophies; a random steering-wheel clock; a bottle opener duct-taped to the server-station railing; cold, no-frills bathrooms with etched and scratched mirrors; and an open-faced tackle box nailed to the wall organizing credit cards and IDs by last-name letter (all patrons running tabs must also fork over their IDs, thanks to some scumbag who ran up a $90 tab on a stolen credit card). A rectangular piece of two-inch-thick plywood resting where the window by the front door should be tells the story of a man who, after being 86'd, returned around 4 a.m., put one of the patio tables through the window (as well as his fist through a POS touch-screen machine), trailed blood through the bar and into the women's bathroom (where he apparently fell and rolled around in it) and scared the Spanish-speaking shit out of a cleaning lady, who eventually found the courage to call her bilingual husband to make the 911 call. As of this writing, she is still reluctant to return to work.

## Shuffleboard

**Beer Depot Lounge**

**Candlelight Tavern**

**Don's Club Tavern**

**Retreat Lounge**

**Skylark Lounge**

**Squire Lounge**

## Sancho's Broken Arrow

*741 East Colfax Avenue*
Phone: 303-832-5288

Hipster Scale  Dive Bar Rating

It's not really my scene, but Sancho's deserves a lot of credit for the counter culture it supports: hippies, mostly, though in Colorado the line between hippies and garden-variety, Subaru-driving natives and transplants is so blurred that it's foolish to assume everyone who loves this bar has dreadlocks, unconventional armpit hair or poor hygiene. Around these parts, it's difficult even to categorize fans of jam bands as anything except exactly that—people who like, love or can mostly tolerate ten-minute guitar and drum solos.

Before you visit, ask yourself: Do I fit into the aforementioned category? If the answer is "no," regardless of whether some of your closest friends wear tie-dye and tailgate all three days of Widespread Panic at Red Rocks, you won't make it ten minutes inside Sancho's. Why? Because, with a few exceptions—Jimi Hendrix, Neil Young, the Rolling Stones and Steve Miller Band—the turn-page jukebox is stocked almost exclusively with Grateful Dead albums and bootlegs. (Phish and Widespread also make limited appearances.). And the volume is loud. All the time.

If you're okay with extended guitar noodling and all-out shredding, then by all means float on in. The two-for-one happy hour begins at 4:20 p.m. (see what they did there?); the walls and ceilings are covered in more Dead and Phish posters, photos, mosaics and murals than even heaven on the greatest of acid trips; and three pools tables, two foosball setups and an air hockey table await. No matter how in tune with nature you are, shoes are strongly recommended due to sticky stone floors, sunken steps leading to vomit-caked bathrooms and no less than 300 other feet ready to crush yours on any given night. Yes, the place gets packed, at which point the volume goes up, which leads to outright pandemonium.

The feel-good, extended-solo kind—if that's your scene.

## Satire Lounge

*1920 East Colfax Avenue*
Phone: 303-322-2227

*Hipster Scale*
🥸🥸🥸🥸🥸🥸

*Dive Bar Rating*
🍾 (now)  🍾🍾🍾 (then)

In 1960, so the story goes, Bob Dylan played a set of Woody Guthrie songs at the Satire; Judy Collins is said to have played a few; The Smothers Brothers were first noticed goofing around here and encouraged to do it full time. Such is the folklore.

The beginning of the Pete Contos empire (Pete's Kitchen + seven other joints), the fifty year-old Satire Lounge still retains much of its original charm, most notably in the red vinyl padding of the stools and booths (now with duct tape covering the holes!) and the iconic art-deco neon sign reaching well above the roof. It's one of the few places on this stretch of Colfax where the tenders can not only make your favorite drink (good luck finding a proper Old Fashioned nearby), but have a deliciously nasty habit of making up new drinks on the regular (ask for a Passport—a margarita with a Coronita turned upside down in it). I've seen friends order $5 shots of vodka/Red Bull and get a low ball of well vodka + a full can of Red Bull + an empty glass. Incredible.

Stumble in around the holidays and you'll find Christmas stockings for employees past and present hanging near the bathrooms, which (in the case of the men's) provide a clear shot of whoever's inside every time the lockless doors are opened. Faded and quaintly outdated Colorado sports pennants hang from the ceiling along with other kitsch and crap. In addition to $1 drafts and $1 off everything else during happy hour (Monday-Friday 4-6 p.m.), you can eat $3 burritos and nachos and $1.50 tacos (enjoy a massively tasty Mexican menu until 1:30 a.m. every day).

It was as the end of my first visit to the Satire spiraled toward sizzled senselessness that I discovered its most endearing quality. I had made friends with two guys sitting to my left when one of them pointed to the black-and-white analog clock on the back wall. "Real time, bro," he mumbled. I looked around for another clock but couldn't find one. "I wouldn't shit you," he assured me. "It's the only bar I've ever been in that runs on real time, and I've been in a lot of bars." For a full minute, maybe more, I was the definition of disbelief. With one eye pinched shut, I studied the ticking clock: 1:30 a.m. "So you're telling me that if I look at my cell phone right now, it's going to say 1:30 a.m.?" I asked the bartendress, dumbfounded, "and that you open and close the bar by that clock?" She nodded and smiled. I shook my head in awe and finished my beer. "Incredible."

UPDATE: Between April and May of 2009—five or so months after the original blurb below was written—the Satire underwent major plastic surgery. Walls were knocked down; the torn and tattered replaced with granite and stainless steel; the bathrooms completely overhauled; and hi-dcf TVs hung to a gratuitous degree. But no amount of swank can change this landmark's history. So while, on the surface, everything looks shiny and new, it is still unmistakably the Satire—the drinks are still cheap, the Mexican food still tasty, the last call still the latest in town and the schizophrenics still talking to themselves at the end of the bar. Something tells me that, sooner rather than later, the Satire will dive once again.

## Best Menu (Mexican)

**Brewery Bar II**

**Campus Lounge**

**El Chapultepec**

**Old Curtis Street Bar**

**Satire Lounge**

# Skylark Lounge

*140 South Broadway*
*Phone: 303-722-7844*

*Hipster Scale*

*Dive Bar Rating*

Now comfortably settled into new(ish) digs just three blocks south of its former home for 60 years (and where Barry's on Broadway currently does its damndest to live up to the legend), the Skylark is nothing if not a Denver institution. It's true that the reincarnation is roomier, cleaner and a smidge less rough around the edges, but it's still so goddamn vintage. Bygone motion-picture posters, some of them for films more than 80 years old—think *Hit Parade of 1947*, *St. Louis Blues* (with Bessie Smith), *The Bronze Buckaroo* and *The Outlaw* (with Jane Russell), among many, many others—share every inch of wall space with photographs of actors, musicians, politicians and other limelight types. Cash registers, candy machines, spare vinyl-stocked jukeboxes and tabletop bowling games provide the same sort of nostalgia that a trip to the Yankee Trader does, but without all the clutter and dust. And upstairs in the Pair-o-Dice Poolroom—which, while shiny and new, has made room for pool and shuffleboard tables, similar checkerboard floors and an even cooler compact-disc jukebox than the one a flight down—find old-school Simpsons and Rocky and Bullwinkle pinball machines. Speaking of the jukeboxes: Not only are they stocked with everything from Dwight Yoakam to Elvis Costello to Billie Holiday to the Violent Femmes, but both encourage customers to make suggestions for future inclusions to the barkeep on duty. How cool is that?

Ten beers on tap and a credit-card terminal have made life on the main floor more luxurious, and the wraparound patio nourishes Denver's obsession with outdoor imbibing, but when a roots, rockabilly or alt-country band hits the small corner stage, the 'Lark's home crowd of scooter-tramp greasers and South Broadway hipsters put on their get-drunk-and-get down shoes and harken back to the days when seedy and squalid were its most coveted characteristics.

# William's Tavern

*423 East 17th Avenue*
Phone: 303-861-9813

Hipster Scale
🍸🍸🍸🍸🍸

Dive Bar Rating
🍾🍾

This is how utterly shitfaced our bartender is: He's considerably more drunk than I am, and I'm in 1:30-a.m., slumped-over-the-bar, double-fisting-PBRs kind of shape. But I'm happy, and so is he. I can tell from the way he grins and laughs every time he over-pours one of my buddy's whiskey and sodas, or leans too far into the ice tub, or can't find the right tab on the bar counter and just gives up. He's solid gold.

But he's not an actual employee—he's the bartendress's boyfriend who's been boozing and shooting pool all night but has invited himself behind the bar to help out during the bar-close rush. I know for a fact that the owner wouldn't be pleased with the situation, but we're all getting better service because of him, so fuck it. Two hours ago, my wife, Maggie, and I arrived at William's with every intention of leaving. The plan—as it is every time we start our night here—was to wait for all of our friends to coalesce, have a quick drink and then continue on an informal 17th Avenue bar crawl. But each time we've tried (and this marked our fourth attempt), we've ended up closing the place down, and tonight is no exception.

I have theories about why this happens. Bar games—including darts (my true bar love) and Silver Strike Bowling—play an important role, as does the jukebox (when the staff hasn't pre-loaded ninety minutes of metal). The regular free meals and Sunday hangover brunch—cooked up in a Crock Pot, served with ruffled potato chips—are a definite bonus. "Simpsons" reruns show on weeknights in relative silence. And the black-walled, biker-bar-without-the-bikers atmosphere is perfect for any occasion (I've spent birthdays and New Year's here in complete bliss) But it's not like the drinks are all that cheap ($2.50 for a PBR can, $5 for most mixed drinks) or the digs super comfortable (mismatched tables and chairs make up much of the room). I think what it comes down to is that the best way to drink with friends—whether it's a Sunday-morning Bloody Mary while waiting to get into Bump & Grind (R.I.P.) a few doors down, or a bladdered bloodbath of binge drinking, like it is tonight—is to do so in a spot that's low on pretension and high on charm. Whenever I'm in Uptown, William's is that spot.

## Squire Lounge

*1800 East Colfax Avenue*
Phone: 303-333-9106

*Hipster Scale*
᏶Ᏸ᏶᏶᏶᏶

*Dive Bar Rating*
🍾🍾🍾

The cops are everywhere by the time we roll up to the Squire Lounge just after 8 p.m.—two squads blocking (and facing) eastbound traffic, another pulled halfway onto the sidewalk, all of them screaming red and blue, all of it a familiar and strangely comforting display of Colfax drama at its finest. We linger and gawk for a moment, then head inside to find out what happened.

The story goes like so: Homeless Guy #1 hobbles/half falls in the front door gripping a wooden cane above his head and screaming about needing the police. Then Homeless Dude #2 tears in after him, demanding his stick back. A scuffle ensues. A bartender hops the bullet-shaped bar and bullies them to the curb, where they continue to have at each other. Someone calls the police. Two beats of a vagabond's drum later, five of Denver's finest have their guns drawn and their mad faces on. Yelling and handcuffing breaks out, and then: fire extinguished. Nothing to see here.

Welcome to the Squire, where drag-down skirmishes and verbal altercations between staff, customers, hobos and the 5-0 are not necessarily the rule, but certainly not the exception.

But then, that's why I love this place, this urinal-cake-smelling diamond in the rough: Except in the dead of winter, the front door's always open, which means shenanigans are never more than a few feet from wandering inside and attempting to bum a dollar or get a sip off that pitcher. Always on the alert, the staff is quick to castigate these (mostly) harmless clochards in front of everyone, and while the over-salted shuffleboard table with its scuffed-up, broken pucks is fun (and free), there's nothing better than watching the dirt get swept out the door from the safety of your bar stool.

With the fisticuff fiasco over and PBRs in hand, I proceed to tell a friend about a no-drama night here when Maggie and I parked ourselves at the bar next to a middle-aged man with worry lines etched into his forehead. After exchanging pleasantries, he told us his very sad story—about being from out of town, about his terminally ill son in a bed over at Children's and about his wife's insistence that he go for a walk and find a drink. While talking, this man and my wife simultaneously discovered a $50 bill on the floor by their feet. Is it yours? No. Is it yours? No. Let's drink on it, then; and we all did, until he needed to get back. And though he tried to let us keep the change, we insisted that he take it and buy something for his kid. "Take him somewhere nice when he gets out," we told him with probably false optimism.

I'm damn near weeping into my beer by the time I finish this story, but I'm drunk, and those things have a way of going together. It helps that everything is so fucking cheap (especially on Sunday nights, when you can bring $10 and forget that you came) and perfect for memory loss—like the Bionic Beaver. Legendary on Colfax, the Beaver is a 52-ounce pitcher filled with whatever the bartender feels like including—rums, vodkas, beers, juices, whatever—and served with a handful of straws. It's notorious for both beginning and ending nights, sometimes simultaneously.

Good morning and good night.

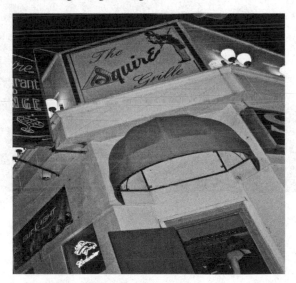

Carioca Café  (Bar Bar)

# DOWNTOWN DENVER

# Carioca Café (Bar Bar)

*2060 Champa Street*                    *Hipster Scale*        *Dive Bar Rating*

*Phone: 303-296-1250 7AM CASH*

The bummer about Bar Bar (officially the Carioca Café) is not that the bathrooms are glacial, grimy, graffiti-covered dungeons. It's not that the volatile mix of white, black, brown and out-of-town patrons are wont to drink until an altercation seems like a good idea. It's not even that the torn booth padding and worn-down-to-the-wood stools are uninviting and sad. The bummer is that within the next seven years—what's left on a ten-year lease—Bar Bar will likely be gone.

Downtown Denver will eventually be as Starbucked and condo-fucked as Seattle, only with more sunshine. But times, thank God, are tough. If you're Tim Fink, who's been part owner of Bar Bar for the past six years and continues to tend bar here despite having only five fingers, this country's current state of economic ruin means two separate but equally promising things: The landlords won't be dozing the block's only remaining edifice to build big-ticket residences any-time soon, and Bar Bar business—thanks to bargain-basement booze prices—should be booming.

Pabst drafts at Bar Bar are always $2; buckets of four mix-and-match domestic bottles are $10. From 7 a.m. until noon, ten-ounce Pabst draws are a buck, Eye Openers (any draw and a three-quarters shot) ring in at $2.25, and tall Bloody Marys feel exorbitant at $3. Three daily happy hours—7 to 9 a.m., 4 to 6 p.m. and 10 p.m. to mid-night—offer first-drink twofers on everything except pitchers. Tip-plers who only feel like one can let someone else cash in their wooden nickel (a tiny plastic shot cup) or put their name on the saved-drink list tacked to the office door—any name with two or more tallies carries over indefinitely (single savers disappear every seven days).

Crazy-cheap suds aren't the only reason to celebrate one of downtown's few remaining dives. In fact, for visitors willing to put up with (or better, embrace) the occasional slurred advance or screaming match, Bar Bar has something for almost everyone. The music spectrum ranges from open-floor (there's no stage) blues jams on Monday nights to live bands (though they occasionally don't show) on weekends and one of Denver's better compact-disc jukes all the time. In the back, a cork dartboard adjacent to the women's bathroom keeps the rare female on her toes (of the predominantly male demographic, Fink says, "This is mostly a guy bar, but it ain't a gay bar!"); Ms. Pac Man, Galaga and an Indianapolis 500 pinball machine offer nostalgia for spare change; and a perpetually breaking air hockey table and a pool table are just a service window away from refills. Unlike many a neighborhood joint in this town, Bar Bar hasn't replaced its fat-back televisions with flatter, more highly defined screens, but the local games are always on, and classic Westerns often play during off-hours.

And then there's Bar Bar's decor: Hundreds and hundreds of color three-by-fives Scotch-taped to every which wall show patrons smiling, shouting and sleeping; the south wall above the booths displays an impressive array of beer (Heineken, Stroh's, Miller Reserve) and booze (Cuervo, Beefeater, Glenfiddich) mirrors; and the ledge above the bar flaunts an unparalleled collection of kitsch and assorted other crap—flags, a wooden Nutcracker, sports cards, a Cat in the Hat lunchbox, a Betty Boop doll, mannequin heads—all coated in a thick level of dust and debris.

If it seems totally fucked that Bar Bar may perish at the first sign of an economic upswing—and that high-rise lobbies and fitness rooms will soon outnumber saloons here on the far edge of downtown—that's because it is. Maybe Fink can somehow outsmart this paradox and emerge with his tavern intact. If not?

Well, here's to being broke but drunk right now.

# El Chapultepec

*1962 Market Street*

*Phone: 303-295-9126  8AM CASH*

*Hipster Scale*

*Dive Bar Rating*

Sinatra, Bennett, Fitzgerald, Miles Davis. McCartney, Jagger, Bono, Harry Connick Jr. They've all played here, so it goes. Even Denver's favorite beatnik, Jack Kerouac, allegedly slept it off in his car outside but came in to clean up in the bathrooms. Mention El Chapultepec around these parts and the names of famous musicians rumored to have graced the tiny corner stage rain down like ten-ton cinderblocks. Take two tiny steps through the front door and into the narrow, 49-person-capacity front room, however, and your gut reaction is liable to be disbelief with a splash of amazement.

For fifty-plus years and counting, the 'Pec's red-and-white checkered tile floor, plaster walls and flimsy wooden stage have undulated with both locally and nationally celebrated jazz. Seven nights a week. With no cover. These days, the weekly lineup leans more toward blues than jazz, but the latter will always play a central role in this institution's reputation. Outside, the paint is flaking and the iconic neon BAR/CAFÉ/CANTINA sign is rusting and burned out (in places) as often as it's lit. But inside, brand new carpet on the stage and fake-brick paneling along the three back walls indicate a promising future. (The last time the stage area—where a plastic fishbowl labeled "requests" atop a piano and a full drum kit are near-permanent fixtures—was "remodeled" in any way was almost 20 years ago, when dirty carpet was both laid and hung.)

El Chapultepec's 34-person-capacity back room—the café— serves up a moderate-sized Mexican menu highlighted by spicy green chili and a ground beef burrito (or Mexican hamburger—whatever you prefer). An S-shaped Formica bar separates the mostly exposed kitchen from a few booths, an awkwardly placed pool table and two tube television showing nothing in particular (unless the home team is playing).

Every day from open until 9 p.m. (when the band starts), happy hour prices reign supreme; the smattering of daytime bar flies, regulars and transients drink $1.50 Coors drafts or wells for a few quarters more. Once the instruments are tuned and the high hat splashing, a series of signs in all directions enforce the basics: "One Drink Minimum Per Set" (though sometimes it's two); "No Dancing" (not strictly enforced, though there typically isn't room to do more than bounce and sway); and "Water For Paying Customers Only. We Sell Bottled Water $2.00."

When the Rockies are home, El Chapultepec is post-game ground zero (a minor leaguer could chuck a ball from the 'Pec's front door through the admission turnstiles behind home plate), so plan to arrive early if you hope for a drink, let alone a view of the stage. On most other nights, 8 or 8:30 p.m. are safe bets for a seat in a booth or at the bar. But why wait? Show up for grub before sundown, slurp down some of downtown's cheapest suds and soak in a one-of-a-kind experience.

# Herb's

*2057 Larimer Street*
*Phone: 303-299-9555*

*Hipster Scale*

*Dive Bar Rating*

Brian, Matt and I are already good and stumbly by the time we fall into the dim red glow of Herb's (Hideout) via the back patio door. And although seventeen different bottles and six different taps taunt us, we all agree that cheap beers are in order. Three PBR cans, two bucks each.

With the exception of the jukebox—which, throughout the course of any given night might play everything from Alicia Keys to Tom Jones to Billy Idol to Nirvana to Christina Aguilera to Out-Kast—the place is pretty quiet. The stillness is rare: Besides a dark, no-frills ambience and well-poured drinks, what Herb's does best is live blues, jazz and open stage that attracts drifters, hipsters and the inconspicuously beautiful alike.

There aren't three vacant stools at the bar, so we grab a tiny table in front of the stage area, just off the dance floor. Directly above, a disco ball spins without incandescent purpose. To our right, a group of six or seven girls take an AC/DC song as their cue to pace around like ducks and bang their elbows in ironic gestures of amusement. We sip (and spill) our PBRs and take stock of how much this section of Herb's feels like a low-rent, ramshackle strip joint without poles: The tables are small and sticky, the metal-framed chairs padded, the entire back wall one large mirror. Probably doesn't help that as a Too $hort song comes on, a spectacle breaks out on the stage. One girl, a brunette wearing a Rockies hat, grabs a long orange extension cord, wraps it around her waist and swings it seductively. Off to the side, another girl sits in a chair while a third girl thrusts her crotch back and forth within licking distance of the seated girl's face. All three are fully clothed, all hysterical with laughter. Even on off nights, the energy in this dive rarely ebbs.

The patio—all white resin chairs, black metal tables and red plastic ashtrays—is empty, and for good reason. I get no more than three or four sips into my pint of Boddingtons ($3 You Call It on Mondays) before the sky starts spewing big, stupid raindrops on us, despite any discernible presence of rain clouds. Brian and Matt scurry inside, but

I have three-quarters of a smoke left, so I hover by the closed-down service window and try to stay dry. During the summer, a grill pours smoke and serves up delectables nearly every night while the party rages on inside. No such luck tonight. Just when I think I can't handle another raindrop, the bartender peeks his head out the back door, points a remote control toward the sky and commands a green automatic awning to unroll itself and save me from drowning. I clap and cheer; he responds with equally puckish and foursquare bravado, saying, "Shit, man, that's just how I roll!"

Back inside, Brian, Matt and I spend a buck each and do battle, Silver Strike 2009 style. We bet rounds of drinks on single frames, regularly pausing the game because one or another of us is helping the bartender and a few strangers play nudie Photo Hunt on the touch screen console. In the end, I lose terribly—my score an embarrassing 108, due mostly to my inability to accurately count pins with both eyes open. After closing out our tabs, we stumble for the diamond-plated bathroom and take turns at the sole urinal while an embarrassed defecator struggles to keep the lockless stall door closed with his hand, then finally stumble out the back door whence we came.

## Best Menu (General)

**Barricuda's**

**Charlie Brown's Bar & Grill**

**Club 404**

**Gabor's**

**Park Tavern & Restaurant**

# My Brother's Bar

2376 15th Street
Phone: 303-455-9991

Hipster Scale

Dive Bar Rating

As the oldest joint in town still serving alcohol on the original site, My Brother's Bar, the Denver landmark that it is, would seem to need no introduction or explanation. Who, after all, has lived in these parts more than a few minutes without either visiting or being urged to? Is anyone reading this from the comfort of their suburban home and yelling, "Hey honey? Have you ever heard of this place?" I should hope not. Still, there's no foul in simply not having gotten down to 15th and Platte and inside this former Beat hangout—see the framed letter Neal Cassady wrote from his reformatory room about an outstanding tab—especially considering there's never been a sign and the enormous REI overshadows every other building in the area.

First and foremost, newbies should know that it's probably not what most barflies would consider a dive. The building is obviously real damn old, and the crown molding, stained-glass windows, low lighting, wooden surfaces and tumbledown tables—not to mention antique fixtures and cash register—maintain a swagger of grizzled jurisdiction. But the crowds (and there are usually crowds) come for the big-ticket burgers served in wax paper and accompanied by clever condiment corrals; they come for the Girl Scout Cookies, sold by the caseload when in season; and they come for the naturally shaded beer garden, known to imbibe until the wee hours of the weekends. The fact is that the crowds come day or night, and they can afford the $4-5 microbrews and imports so expertly poured from the taps. These aspects don't disqualify a legendary joint from consideration, obviously, but—as with the Cherry Cricket or the Wazee Supper Club, most notably—they cannot be ignored.

My Brother's Bar has no bottled beer (who needs it with these draft options?), no jukebox (classical music only, though the roar of conversation almost always overpowers it), no televisions (talk with someone!), no menus (it's all on chalkboards) and very little in the way of cutlery and china (no plates, not ever). It usually has popcorn, perfect for devouring while waiting (and you will usually wait) for the grease-soaked food to arrive. And it most certainly has history. Loads of it.

Stop in and make some of your own.

# Old Curtis Street Bar

2100 Curtis Street          Hipster Scale      Dive Bar Rating
Phone: 303-292-2083

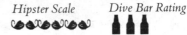

Probably my favorite thing about the Old Curtis Street is the clock behind the bar. Sounds weird, I know, especially considering the clock isn't anything special in and of itself—it's not vintage, valuable, made from crack cocaine...nothing. It's just a clock. Except that the numbers are reversed, so that clockwise of 12 is 11 instead of 1 (and so on all the way around). I love this because I've been shitfaced here countless times without noticing. It took a sober visit on a tranquil Tuesday evening for me to see it for what it truly is: a really clever trick. I laughed out loud at the idea of other Denver drunks losing all sense of time and place while glancing at it—and blaming those nine $1 draws and three shots of Crown for their disorientation. Well played, sirs.

Pete Razatos—a gruff old Greek guy who, on my sober visit, played the vintage Double Up poker machine silently in a well-pressed button-up and vest as his bartendress washed glasses—opened this warm, wood-paneled neighborhood joint in 1976. Five years ago, his son, Kosta, gave up a job trading futures on the Chicago Mercantile Exchange to move back and run the place when pops threatened to sell it. What's the same is that the kitchen still kicks out tasty, affordable Mexican grub; the jukebox is still loaded with Queen, the Beatles, Bowie, the Latin Oldies Trilogy, Elvis, Sly and the Family Stone and Zeppelin; the maroon vinyl booths and padded chairs don't look a day over 30; and the cash register, blender and annunciator panel (fire and theft protection), well, they're the same. Since opening day, it seems. The whole place is pretty dated, actually—down to the black-and-white photos of old Denver lining the walls. Which is great. Really great.

What's new is that local rock bands, comedians, artists and other entertainers are using the small stage (obstructed, unfortunately, by a bulky pillar and suspended speaker) no less than three nights a week; the space has been widely accepted as a great place for large groups (wedding after-parties, happy-hour meet-ups, birthday parties) to meet; and the Razatos installed a much-needed (and spacious) side patio. Which is also great.

Really great.

# Shelby's Bar & Grill

*519 18th Street*
*Phone: 303-295-9597*

Hipster Scale

🍸🍸

Dive Bar Rating

🍺🍺

Though I've been unable to verify it in any empirically responsible way, I hear *Esquire* magazine dubbed Shelby's the "Cheers of Denver." Hmph. I'm not sure I could disagree more, so I'm going to go ahead and safely file this adorable quotable under Hyperbole and move on.

Housed in a building dating back to 1906, Shelby's is the 6th in a long line of businesses that have occupied this address, including a mortuary (it's also haunted!), a couple Italian eateries and a few saloons rumored to have been speakeasies (secret underground passageways connect it to all of downtown!). Okay, okay: You caught me. I got all that from the back of the menu.

Here it is, sans superlatives: Shelby's is a nice little dive on the edge of downtown's business district. It does a mean lunch hour for the monkey suit/cubicle set, an even stronger early-evening happy hour (4-6:30 p.m.; two-for-one domestics and double cocktails for the single price) and has been known to heat up for its late-night happy hour (11 p.m.—1 a.m.; same deals). Unless something special's going on, Saturdays are slow and it's closed on Sundays. Prices are fair: Most beers hover near $3, while well and wine ring up at $3.50-$4.00. The two-page menu is reasonably diverse, though you can rarely go wrong with a burger and a pile of half-moon home fries.

But only if Tim Burton re-imagined NBC's Boston-based situation comedy as film noir would I be comfortable with the "Cheers" comparison. I see the covered, full-rectangle-shaped bar similarity, but everything else about Shelby's—from the ripped and torn padding on everything to the crumbling, run-down faux-Formica-paneled bathrooms (with white plastic buckets for garbage cans) to the impenetrable layer of grime on the condiment bottles—is much too coarse for prime time.

# Tarantula Billiards

*1456 Champa Street*
Phone: 720-932-6666

Hipster Scale

Dive Bar Rating

I enter Tarantula Billiards and traipse up its steep case of wooden stairs for the first time with an unbelievable streak going—I haven't puked in 10 years. I barrel down the stairs of Tarantula Billiards three hours later and projectile vomit 180 degrees of carnage all over Champa Street. You'd think I'd be disappointed, but the only taste left in my mouth after the experience is admiration. The Tarantula was able to do what a thousand bars before it couldn't: humble me. I have returned many times for this reason, and for the air hockey.

This night, a dozen friends and I roll in on a mission. We push three tall tables together in the bar area and listen as a DJ spins non-stop electronica (quite a paradoxical dichotomy, this place: divey pool hall meets after-dark club). Like a bunch of drunks in a penny arcade, we bruise up our knuckles with fervent enthusiasm and spend a small fortune working the room's lone air hockey table. At one point, I knock an entire pint of Bud onto the blue and silver surface and watch in blasted awe as the liquid bubbles and sizzles in the artificial air. Those who stay back at the tables are treated to pastel-colored roses by the owner.

Downtown's best no-bullshit pool hall—17 nine-foot-long slate tables sit on original hardwood floors in a rectangular room with brick walls and wide windows overlooking the city—offers stick shooters free play all day so long as they're drinking or eating (after 7 p.m. on weekends the price is a measly $3/hour per person). The menu is diverse – burgers, sandwiches, pizza, wings— and delicious, and drinks are expertly poured; not exactly a tough sell.

While the bar is long and the drinks strong, there's no table service; when the place is packed, players often have to pause their games for ten minutes at a time while they wait for a pour. The overly concerned—you know who you are, two-piece-cue-plus-case owners—might as well save their skills for the daylight hours. Show up after dark for the beats and booze. And if you're lucky, a slice of humble pie.

## Star Bar

*2137 Larimer Street*
Phone: 303-292-0029  *CASH*

*Hipster Scale*

*Dive Bar Rating*

I'm just starting to peel back the label on my third Bud when Terry slides onto the stool next to me at the last great dive on Larimer Street. I'm at Star Bar to watch the Rockies; Terry's here because he works at a game-day parking lot down the street, and because pitchers are always six bucks. During a commercial, I overhear him griping to Dina, our bartendress, about how the $60 he gets paid each shift isn't worth the middle fingers and verbal harassment he receives from stingy drivers. "Got spit on twice tonight," he says matter-of-factly. "Ain't the first time."

I've met all sorts of characters while drinking at Star Bar—some friendly, some not. There was Max, who could hardly stand without wobbling but still managed to dance by himself on the abandoned dance floor before he started a fight and was hustled out by Scott, the bar's elderly manager and de facto bouncer. There was the one-legged guy in a wheelchair who wanted to talk baseball over a smoke, and who later wheeled himself up to the table my friends and I were all sitting around to finish the conversation. My favorite, however, was the woman in sweatpants and flip-flops who bummed a dollar off me to buy a beer and proceeded to tell me her life story, a sweet-in-a-sad-kind-of-way tale that ended with her smiling nervously and saying, "So, basically, I'm not happy. Sorry for unloading. Thanks for listening."

Sometime between my second and third beer tonight, I see Scott—who wears a dirty green hat embroidered with a gold star and the word "Bar" next to it—once again throwing around his grandfatherly muscle. "After the first of the year," he hollers at some drunk (it's October). "That's when you can come back. After the first of the year." This time he's not hollering at Max, who's back at a table by the dance floor, looking significantly more sober than he was the last time we met but wearing the same yellow shirt. Wheelchair Guy is also in attendance, and we again trade pleasantries and talk sports over a cigarette. Missing is the sweet woman in the sweatpants, but I barely notice her absence because I'm too busy talking with Terry.

"Don't see too many other gringos in here," Terry says during another mid-inning commercial. I smile and nod, having noticed this before. We appear to be the only native English speakers in the room besides Scott, though I can't be sure. Almost everyone else—including the guy next to me, who never takes his eyes off the TV because he has $1,500 riding on the game—orders their drinks in Spanish and cheers like it's Mexican Independence Day every time the Rockies score.

It's not until the sixth inning or so that Terry tells me he's been living on the street for the past few months. He has one of those domino-effect self-destruction stories: First his car gave out, then he lost his job as a painter in Commerce City, then he was thrown out of his place on Walnut Street, and finally, his girl left him. But he held down a reasonably steady job all summer and hopes to paint again (his trade for twenty-plus years) once he's squirreled away enough money to get back on his feet. He doesn't use drugs or drink booze on the street, and cites his college-age daughter—who doesn't know he's homeless—as his inspiration to stay clean. He has a dog, an eighteen-month-old bulldog-mastiff mix named Buster, who snuggles with him at night and "is a household name down at Jesus Saves." And if all else fails, this winter he'll catch a bus to Florida, where he has a brother. "I won't be down for long, man," he says, eyes glowing. "And when I'm back up, I'm going to leave my pack by my door as a reminder of where I've been."

What strikes me most about Terry is not how together and responsible he seems, but how generous he is, considering how little he has. Before my fourth Bud is gone, he offers me a glass from his pitcher; before he knows that I smoke, he offers me one of his. I need to leave, but I feel bad saying no, so I accept his offers and stay for another half-inning. When my glass is empty, I order a final pitcher from Dina, place it in front of him and say goodbye with a firm handshake and a warm smile.

# Wazee Supper Club

*1600 15th Street*
*Phone: 303-623-9518*

*Hipster Scale*

*Dive Bar Rating*

Opened in 1954, then purchased in 1974 by the same duo responsible for My Brother's Bar and now owned by Wynkoop Holdings, the Waz is one of Lodo's greatest leftovers—leftover from the Skid Row smog and filth, the abandoned warehouses and squatters, the 15th Street Viaduct that used to pass overhead. The clientele isn't exactly like the regulars of yesteryear (employees from the now-disappeared Post Office Terminal and other industrial sectors), but they've got their heads screwed on a lot straighter than the fauxhawks and miniskirts paying $400 for bottle service a few blocks away.

Pizza may be this joint's claim to fame (love it or hate it), but it's the piecemeal art deco-meets-'50s décor that will make you feel like never leaving: black-and-white checkered tile floors, gas lights from 19th century Milwaukee, the 80-year-old telegraph clock behind the bar, the wooden benches with red padding from the former Denver Elks Club. The cream of the antique crap, however, is the 1930s warehouse-opener-turned dumbwaiter that sends plates and drinks from the kitchen to the lofted second floor (capacity: 50). Watching it work is entertaining; watching its contents topple to the floor below is worth the 20 (or more) minute wait any time the Avs are playing at the Pepsi Center.

With only 10 seats at the bar (and the seat closest to the open kitchen too hot for comfort; seriously), you'll likely find yourself standing or at one of the dining-room tables. The staff can be raucous, is always fun loving and funky, and will buy you a round if you're not a waste of valuable barstool real estate. The kitchen's open 'til 1 a.m. six nights a week (11 p.m. on Sundays) and features a menu worth repeat visits. The newish flatscreen TVs keep sports fans happy without ruining anything. And the classic pull-bar cigarette machine by the bathrooms has a credit card reader attached.

Everything old is new again.

**Berkeley Inn**

# WEST DENVER

# Ace-Hi Tavern

*1216 Washington Avenue, Golden*    *Hipster Scale*    *Dive Bar Rating*
Phone: 303-279-9043   7AM

Despite attempts at one time or another to be historic and touristy like Aspen or competitive and contemporary like Boulder, Golden today remains a small town within commuting distance of Denver —a college town with twenty-somethings binge-drinking on loan money, an industry town with third-shift workers and a whole mess of Coors Brewing Co. employees in dire need of a 7 a.m. cocktail before it's time for some shuteye. For better or worse, Golden is these people, and the Ace-Hi serves them without judgment or reservation.

For the past 130 years a bar has stood at 1216 Washington Avenue, more than 60 of 'em as the Ace. Inside its angled wooden entranceway (soon to be replaced with glass) are all the amenities of a down-home dive—carpet and wood paneling, vinyl padded booths and a well-worn billiards table, NASCAR pools and a spindle brimming with sticky notes declaring who's been 86'd and for what reasons. A triple-rack pizza oven with a fancy new baking stone dishes up frozen Tombstone brand pies for six and eight bucks, while a handful of pickled goodies (turkey gizzards, eggs) run a dollar or less. With weekday happy hours from 7-11 a.m. and 3-8 p.m. serving $1.50 pints and $5 pitchers, and $2 shot specials (Jager! Jameson! Cuervo! McGillicuddy's!) every night but Thursday—not to mention a slew of other discounts for the weary wallet—I always leave feeling like I owe someone an apology. Plus, you can pay with credit now, so long as you drink an Andrew Jackson's worth.

Most endearing, however, are the people—the way they drink and talk like family, if only distant cousins.

On attire: "Mikey, ya got socks and shoes on. What's the occasion?"

On leaving: "Quitter!" "Boo!" "Who needs ya?"

On remodeling the front door:

"Why they putting in glass doors?"

"So people don't walk by and assume this place is just a dingy shithole."

"But this place *is* a dingy shithole!"

"Not for long. Going to be bright as shit in here with them new doors."

"At least we'll be able to see the parades go by."

(All together) "Hooray!"

The Ace, for what it's worth, is not a dingy shithole. Not even close. Students from the School of Mines come in for beer pong and four-way shots off the top of a downhill ski. The old guys, the contractors, the swing shifters—they come 'cause it's cheap and it's close.

We all come for the camaraderie.

## Karaoke

**Bulldog Bar**

**Dr. Proctor's Lounge**

**Hangar Bar**

**Music Bar**

**Ogden Street South**

## Berkeley Inn

*3834 Tennyson Street   7AM*
*(No phone)*

Hipster Scale

Dive Bar Rating

The tower of 30 or more cig cartons behind the bar is hard to miss, but how, exactly, the 63 year-old Berkeley Inn pulls off a cigar-bar exception is still beyond me. Is the entire neighborhood stopping in to buy (what must feel like) tax-free $5 packs? Is the liquor business so slow that a full 5% of revenue is coming from the cancer sticks? However it works, I'm glad it does—I'm not looking to become one of the wrinkle cheeks embalming themselves at the bar, but I do love to light up inside. Occasionally.

Historically a biker bar, in March of 2009 the Berzerkeley came under new ownership, though it never closed during the transition. Some new upholstery on the bar stools and a better booze selection is about all that changed, which means longtime regulars should have little to complain about. Still incredibly in place is the bug zapper for fruit flies; the large, plastic sneeze guard over the open ice chest of domestic beer cans and bottles; the comically massive, second-generation Rock-Ola jukebox with blaring speakers that drown out conversation by the pool table; and the framed photos of regulars. Even the six or so square tables with plastic tops and outdated ads underneath remain, still accompanied by black, plastic stackable chairs.

The first major renovation, should one ever occur, will likely involve the men's bathroom, where the door bangs against the sink, and the toilet and urinal are so close together that simultaneous use is all but impossible. When I mention this detail to the bartender, he tells a handful of stories involving old dudes dropping trow to let loose while he's already in there. "You'd think they'd look away," he exclaims incredulously, "but no! They stare right at my dick!" He's also had a few guys come out and comment, "Your can reminds me of the joint." Um, yeah.

On the mirror behind the bar, dry-erase marker is used to advertise specials and happy hours (7-11 a.m. and 4-7 p.m.—two-for-one). And though an aging ventilation system hums loudly when the jukebox is silent, the noise is a small price to pay for the pleasure of itchy eyes and a nicotine hangover. Oh, how I miss thee.

# Casa Bonita

*6715 West Colfax Avenue, Lakewood*
*Phone: 303-232-5115*

*Hipster Scale*

*Dive Bar Rating*

Casa Bonita is quite obviously Denver's diviest alcohol-serving, indoor amusement park. If you haven't been, or have only seen the "South Park" episode spoofing the 35 year-old, 52,000 square-foot, Mexican-themed restaurant and fun-house-shit-show, I dare say you haven't lived. But not really.

There's no cover, but because there's a 30-foot waterfall with cliff divers (high schoolers in Speedos); a "500-pound" gorilla named Chiquita (another high schooler in a suit) that escapes and gallops around the restaurant; regular shoot-em-ups between the sheriff and "Bad Guy Black Bart" (why's he gotta be black?); strolling maria-chi musicians (tip 'em and they'll never go away); and lost caves and caverns, among other super ridiculous shit, you have to purchase a $12-$15 meal to get in. The rumors are rampant, but if you haven't heard, the food is brutal. Really. So either order randomly and don't eat, or go for the nachos, which are reasonably edible.

When you get to the table, order 2 beers at a time, and don't bother with the Casaritas—they're weak. If you're in a small group and want to wander around together, pound as many beers as you can stomach before leaving the table, because you can't leave the table unattended and you can only get drinks while there. You could al-ways order two beers right before paying and double-fist for the first 10 minutes of walking around, but the best plan is to roll in with a posse and leave the table in shifts.

Once you've ventured out, gotten lost, hit your head inside Black Bart's Cave, had your likeness butchered by the caricature art-ist, gotten lost, knocked over a couple kids (accidentally!) and seen what passes for a puppet show, spend the rest of your time in one of the arcades, where all of the games are Chuck E. Cheese castaways and there's a good chance the attendees will be completely out of tokens. Everywhere. (True story.) If you do find tokens, buy at least a Hamilton's worth and play Skee-Ball for a couple hours. You'll be singing CasaBo's praises for years to come.

But not really.

# Edgewater Inn

*5302 West 25th Avenue, Edgewater*
Phone: 303-237-3524

Hipster Scale    Dive Bar Rating

In the character + atmosphere category, some dives are great precisely because they're so scuzzy and raw, because of their almost comical state of disrepair—they remind you that low overhead = cheap drinks and no bullshit. Others work so well because the wood paneling and carpet (and Naugahyde and Formica…) conjure basements or rec rooms from decades past—and this feels safe, familiar, comforting in a Freudian way. Once in a great while, however, a dive just feels downright cozy. The lighting is warm, the wood well worn, the furnishings cluttered but not cramped. Loud, rowdy and crowded, but still kid friendly. The Edgewater Inn, a mainstay in the quaint little Edgewater neighborhood (town, technically) just west of Sloan's Lake since 1953, is just such a place.

Famous for its pizza (I'd put the hand-tossed Sweetness up there with much of the Chicago deep dish I grew up on, but everyone's a critic: Try it yourself and decide), the Edgewater offers so much more. Order a Moscow Mule—squeezed lime, ginger beer and vodka, served in a copper beggar's cup—here and you'll hesitate before ordering it anywhere else (though Herb's comes in a close second) or, god help you, attempting it at home. Draft beer (Coors or Blue Moon) is served in signature schooners—like drinking out of an 18-ounce medieval chalice, only without the torture and chain mail and all that—that all but demand two hands and steady balance. If the thought of tomato juice doesn't frighten you, ask for that Coors "Red" and thank me later.

When you find yourself sitting around the U-shaped bar (better show up early), ask the barkeep to play the dice game. For a buck, you get 3 rolls of five dice to either hit five of a kind (for the progressive pot) or a full house/four of a kind/straight (for a free well drink or schooner). The only time I've ever played I rolled four 1s; the guy next to me rolled two full houses in a row.

In the small main dining room, green-padded booths (each designated by a house address number nailed into the wood) wrap around the bar and face the kitchen, which is separated by swinging saloon-style doors and which emits a ding! when food orders are ready. Past the bathrooms (clean) and coat racks is a homey outdoor smoking area with lounge furniture and end tables. A sizable side room/patio offers overflow seating and a limited second bar.

And on Sundays during football season, stumble in for lunch and enjoy a Bloody Mary bar ($3 for well, $5 for premium) and a $5 ride to the Broncos game on the "famous" Howdy Bus (it's $10 if you just want the ride sans lunch). You could do a lot worse.

UPDATE: As of early summer 2009, the Edgewater no longer offers the dice game. According to a bartendress, a former, apparently very bitter, employee called the cops and buzzkilled the whole enterprise. Good going, asshole.

**Legal Smoking Inside**

**Berkeley Inn**

**Grizzly Rose**

**Beer Depot**

**Bushwacker's**

**Charlie Brown's (covered/heated patio)**

# Hill-Top Tavern

*4907 Lowell Boulevard 9AM CASH*        *Hipster Scale*        *Dive Bar Rating*
Phone: 303-455-9756                              👓                     🍺🍺🍺

The Hill-Top Tavern will not run a tab for anyone. I know this because a sign taped behind the bar says so. Other signs, some written in Sharpie on scraps of cardboard and paper, some typed but so yellow they look like they were hunted, pecked and printed from a Commodore 64: "We Do Not Accept Credit Cards," "Pitcher Beer Special /$5.00 ea/Mon-Fri/9:30 pm to 1:30 am/Bud + Bud Light + Busch" and, by the pay phone in the corner, "Please Keep Calls Short. Thank you!" Hanging just below this request is a handwritten addendum: "Do Not Answer Phone." Why the thing still rings (and it does), I have no idea.

Split into two rooms—one with pool tables, the other with booths, video games, the juke and the bar—the Hill-Top caters to blue-collars and Regis University students, though the latter typically only swarms at night. I'm told by a reliable source (her mom and dad met here) that Bill Murray, a Regis alum, drinks within these walls when he's in town. Old friends clearly meet here—one man in a navy-blue sweatshirt and massive mustache swings open the front door, drops the case holding his two-piece billiards cue and hollers at a familiar face at the other end of the room, "I knew your ass would be in here tonight! How the hell you been?"

My favorite visit on memory was with a gaggle of friends out to celebrate my birthday. As we entered, one of three gentlemen sitting in silence and watching nothing in particular on the dust-covered tubes eventually poured us $7 pitchers of Bud and two consecutive four-finger vodka-cranberrys with itty-bitty winged critters floating in them: The cran, he eventually discovered, had gone to the fruit flies. We all laughed, nearly choking on the charm. From down the bar, a regular leaned in our direction: "So, other than the bugs, how's your night going?"

Some advice: If the pages on the jukebox jam, first pick songs —say, Queen, Elton John, Bowie—from the visible choices; then enter number combinations at random until the credits are exhausted. Whatever you do, don't bitch. If you can stomach shitty beer, go for

Busch—draws are $1.25, pints $1.75, pitchers $5.50. When it's time to use the can, be warned that the presence of soap, water pressure, and a working light switch should never be assumed. Three types of jerky, assorted nuts and a variety of bagged chips, however, are a given.

And on your birthday? Call ahead and ask for Lyle: He'll serve up an overflowing low ball's worth of your chosen poison, pour the first shot and leave you the rest. On the house.

# King's Court

*1000 South Federal Boulevard*
*Phone: 303-936-1028 7AM CASH*

Hipster Scale 👄👄

Dive Bar Rating

"Be nice to your bartender," says the sign behind the bar at King's Court. "Even a toilet can take only (1) one asshole at a time." This statement pretty much sums up the Court's ethos: no bullshit. Unless, of course, a thunderstorm forces you to park your Road King next to the pool table, and you decide to start it, back it up and ride it out the side door. That, apparently, is perfectly okay. As is the smell of gas and smoke that permeates for a good five minutes afterward (I seemed to be the only one who noticed).

Other signs: "Just because I don't care doesn't mean I don't understand;" "This is your brain (pic of Broncos helmet), This is your brain on drugs (pic of Raiders helmet);" and, on the Red Bull chalkboard, "VIP 5/24: Bud & Rick." As it turns out, all it takes to become a VIP is to write your name and phone number (if you need a call) on a scrap of paper and toss it into the white Styrofoam bowl behind the bar. Each day, the tender pulls two names and the winners get their first drinks free and happy hour prices all day.

At a table in the back, a group of bikers in Canadian tuxedos sat beneath a neon Stroh's sign and tapped along to the country and western crooning from the jukebox speakers. They ate cashews, Hot Tamales and Lotsa Sours from the red, turn-crank vending machines. The bartendress joined them, pulling quarters from her tip bucket to subsidize her snacking.

The bar area was crowded when I arrived for Sunday happy hour, so I grabbed a table next to a side bar with carpet-covered legs, atop which sat a 45-inch rear-projection television kept from falling over screen-first by 4 long pieces of twine tied to hooks in the dark wood-paneled wall. Within eyeshot, I counted at least six different kinds and colors of bar stools and five different types of chairs. Later, a group of employees (regulars?) grabbed these stools by the half dozen, tipped them upside down on the pool tables and tightened all the screws and bolts with drivers and wrenches. This maintenance struck me as the closest thing King's Court has seen to a remodel in a couple decades.

No (bull)shit.

## Live Music

Bulldog Bar

Bushwacker's Saloon

Carioca Café (Bar Bar)

Ease On In Lounge

El Chapultepec

The Grizzly Rose

Hangar Bar

Herb's

Lincoln's Road House

Lion's Lair

Old Curtis Street Bar

Sancho's Broken Arrow

Skylark Lounge

Ziggies

## Micky Manor

*2544 Federal Boulevard*
*Phone: 303-458-0043*

*Hipster Scale*

*Dive Bar Rating*

My inaugural visit to Micky Manor starts out so normal: warm greeting from a group of friends watching the Broncos trail late in the third quarter; pitcher after plastic pitcher of Natural Light ($6), poured steadily into six-ounce glasses and accompanied by complimentary shots of a yellow Kamikaze mixture every time the Broncs score; onion rings, Mexican hamburgers and a slew of greasy firehouse sliders; cheering, booing, laughing, belching. A typical Sunday-afternoon, really.

Then the game ends.

We're sitting at a long, wooden table in the middle of the bar's main room. Couch-comfortable booths line the walls around us, each with its own mirror. As the post-game interviews begin, we reposition our chairs to face each other instead of the TVs and notice a disheveled, dejected-looking woman in a dirty red windbreaker and torn jeans, apparently passed out in a booth by the front door. She's slumped in three or four directions at once—one leg kicking out into open space, the other tucked under the table; her left arm hanging limp by her side, her right cradling her twisted neck. Every few minutes, someone shuffles over to check on her and ask if she's okay. Startled, she nods, garbles an incoherent sentence or two, then goes back to unconsciousness. So we go back to not noticing her. Then, out of nowhere:

"Some fuckin' Whites, huh?" It's our incognizant friend, who is now apparently with it enough to notice us, get up and mumble this under her breath as she stumbles by.

About this time, an AC/DC song comes on, blaring louder than necessary and throwing the whole bar into early-evening drunken pandemonium. That's when we spot her. The other incapacitated woman, the forty-plus-year-old in the too-tight black tank top and low-riding jeans, the one who'd been sitting on the corner stool. Earlier, when I made a sacrificial run for more pitchers, she saw me standing patiently at the end of the bar and, for reasons unknown to me or anyone else sitting near her, threw her whole upper body back, bared all three or four of her teeth and convulsed with unintelligible laughter and chattering.

Now she's on the move, thrusting her crotch at no one in particular, flailing her arms to the ceiling and floor, smearing her ass all over the juke-box glass. We gape in horror and awe as her primary audience—a table full of middle-aged guys decked out in blue and orange—seamlessly transitions from despondently watching their gridiron heroes to exuberantly ogling this inexplicable peep show. The bartendress comes over to clean off our table, and she stares along with us as the former football fans bend and wiggle in their chairs, stand and whoop the dancer on. When the song ends, they beg for more. "Encore!" they wail between whistles. "One more time!" they howl amid claps.

"No, please. Don't," the bartendress says, loud enough for only us to hear.

I'd be a filthy liar if I said this was a one-time occurrence (for a bar with no dance floor, I've never been in without witnessing some sort of spectacle). A Denver institution since 1932—first for the Italians, then the Mexicans—the Manor's first name was originally spelled with a copyright-infringing "e" between the "k" and "y." Even after the wood-paneled watering hole got wise, the neon Micky and Minnie signs hanging in the front windows stayed put. Before closing down for a year between '06 and '07, it was the last place in Colorado to serve (near) authentic Rockybilts (like a slider, but more magical). Order a mixed drink, though, and you'll still get crushed ice. Which isn't exactly normal.

# Music Bar

*4586 Tennyson Street    7AM*          *Hipster Scale*          *Dive Bar Rating*
Phone: 303-458-5360

The problem with karaoke—at least when dealing with hipsters, the creative class or anyone with a college degree, really—is that the whole experience of getting drunk and singing songs from decades past is laced with irony. Especially when a blue-collar bar is involved. "Isn't it so funny," they post to their Facebook pages and blogspots, "that my friends and I sang Prince songs at this seedy karaoke joint last night? Aren't we clever? Just look at these pictures!" Equally irritating is the portrayal of singular karaoke experiences as conversation-stoppingly epic. And while I've definitely experienced more than a few moments of drunken bliss at Music Bar (karaoke every Thursday through Saturday night at 9 p.m.)—for instance, when one friend sang the most amazingly terrifying rendition of "Unchained Melody" that I, or the handful of regulars slow-dancing to it, had ever witnessed—I will not contend their monumental greatness here.

Off the beaten path (and nearly impossible to get a cab from after 1 a.m.), karaoke at Music Bar becomes a tougher sell with every visit. For starters, the party's pretty much always hoppin' on both sides of the bar, which, while amusing to an extent, has a way (at this place) of resulting in shoddy service and strange altercations. Making matters worse, the DJs are prone to saltiness and an inexcusable tendency toward ignoring the growing stack of requests—choosing instead to play long sets of Top 40 hip-hop or classic rock while they talk on their cells or take shots with the bar staff.

Avoid weekend nights, however, and you'll find a well-lit biker dive with sports cards and other Denverabilia lacquered to the tables; a popcorn machine that's rarely empty; saloon-style swinging doors on the bathrooms (for maximum voyeurism); and cheap-ass suds—$5 pitchers and $4 shots on my last visit. Out front, you'll notice a white, spray-painted box extending fifteen feet in every direction to keep smokers away from the door. A bit neurotic, I'd argue, but I suggest complying with local custom.

I once had an incredibly sketchy cabbie drop me off here. For the entire fifteen-minute ride, he screamed at his wife through a cell phone about an impending street fight between his stepdaughter and a girl from her school. "Let those bitches kick each other's asses and go to juvie, for all I care," he shrieked into space. "Fuck it. Going to juvie ain't no big deal. We both did it; so can they." The kicker, though, is what he uttered upon arrival.

"Is this the shithole?"

# Rosa Mia Inn

*4395 Yates Street 8AM CASH*    *Hipster Scale*    *Dive Bar Rating*
Phone: 303-455-9951

I'm locking my scooter to a street sign outside Rosa Mia Inn when the tiny tavern's only patron pops out for a smoke. "You don't need to do that," she informs me. "Everyone in this neighborhood knows each other; no one's going to take it." She proceeds to tell stories of bicycles left leaning against the bar's brick wall and various other vehicles unlocked for hours at a time while the owners were inside. I believe her, but my last ride was ripped off in broad daylight downtown, so I'm not taking any chances.

Opened in 1966 as an Italian hangout for the West Highland and Berkeley neighborhoods, the Rosa Mia originally catered to employees of both Lakeside Amusement Park and the original Elitch Gardens. But with Elitch's now in the Platte Valley and Lakeside only open in the summer (and run predominantly by teenagers), business on the corner of 44th and Yates just isn't the same. Still, if you visit in the morning—doors open at 8 a.m. every day—you'll be served by 91-year-old Julie, who has operated the joint for all of its forty-plus years (she owned it with her sister, who has passed away). If you visit on a Monday, Wednesday or Thursday, Julie will be joined by 88-year-old Kathy, both of them sitting at the far end of the bar, "both of 'em still feisty," according to tonight's bartendress, Sher. As proof, Sher points to a large brown jug on the back counter with a yellow plastic funnel duct-taped to the top, colorful Mardi Gras beads draped all around. "That's Julie's Cuss Bucket," I'm told: Foul mouths pay fifty cents or find somewhere else to drink.

Mounted on the wall to the left of the Cuss Bucket is a pastel-green rotary phone; directly above is a massive vintage Budweiser Clydesdale wagon scene encased in wood and glass. Photographs dating back to the turn of the last century are taped and lacquered to beveled squares of wood hanging on either side of the Clydesdales. On the counter sit a box of Inglenook red wine; an assortment of handles of booze, each with a neon sticker bearing the price per drink; various snack-sized bags of chips, nuts and over-the-counter medications; and an old-school Menumaster Micro-Popper, which doles out popcorn for $1.25. Coffee's on in the corner. My favorite quirk—besides, maybe, the buck's head between the bathrooms or the communal sink and mirror in the main room—has to be the Rosa Mia Open plaque that stops with the 2006 winners, despite the annual golf tournament's continuance. When I wrongly assume the Open is closed, Sher tells me that the guy who did the engraving is in a spat with Julie and refuses to come in or update it.

Rosa Mia's most welcoming quality remains the warm lighting and family-room atmosphere—I'd guess the entire place at maybe 800 square feet, give or take a hundred. The ancient yet classic Megatouch XL Platinum, Four Play and Double Up gaming machines ("for amusement only," says a handwritten message) are a fun touch, as are $2 mugs of Bud and Bud Light (the only brews on tap). And while the Internet jukebox steals quarters and the volume is difficult to manage, a few extra decibels aren't necessarily a bad thing, considering how quiet it's been around here.

## Rustic Tavern

*5126 West 29th Avenue*
*Phone: 303-455-9843  7AM CASH*

Hipster Scale     Dive Bar Rating

Eighty-two year-old JoAnn Turner, who bought the Rustic Tavern with her husband 52 years ago and continues to oversee its daily operations, is showing me her photo albums. There's so-and-so: his dog got hit by a car and we buried it out back; there's Uncle Fred: he bartended here for 10 years and left us $300 when he died so everyone could have a few drinks at his wake; there's so-and-so: she lives in Oklahoma now but still visits; there's Sexy Rexy...

As we flip through page after page, album after album, JoAnn tells me that in all her life, she's never had a drink of alcohol or a drag from a cigarette; that her mother just passed at the age of 101 plus seven months; that her uncle opened the Satire, another family member was involved with Herb's Hideout, another the original Brown Barrel. She shows me so-and-so's funeral program, tucked into the sleeve of the large brown album, and a Rustic Tavern matchbook ("The Friendly Tavern") so old that the phone number is in two-letter plus four-digit format (GL-9843). She shares her entire life with me, and I soak it in along with more $1.75 frosty mugs of Budweiser than I can count.

We gab and gab about her bar, which existed 15 years before she bought it and was a butcher shop before that. I am an inquisitive grandson, desperate for family folklore; she is the matriarch of an extended family so large that five full photo albums can't begin to tell the whole story. While we're rapping, Cathy, the bartendress, leaves to give Jimmy, a regular too drunk to be operating heavy machinery, a ride home. During her absence, JoAnn draws my attention to the cash register (older than the Rustic), the vintage, non-regulation-sized pool table (which she owns and is worth a bundle) and the sign behind the bar that reads, "In God we trust. All others pay cash."

When Cathy returns, we laugh about and lament how the kids who broke the original neon sign by throwing crab apples at it so long ago now come in as adults. They recount the hilarity that ensues at semi-annual, decorate-your-own lampshade-wearing parties and potluck dinners. They give me a tour of the new backyard/patio area, which features a bamboo fence and electronic tiki torches; full, low-hanging trees; green grass (and a dog grave); and a few tables crafted from large wooden cable spools. I sink into a patio chair, light up a smoke and never want to leave.

## Squeeze Inn

*5395 West 48th Avenue*
*Phone: 303-458-6440   7 AM*

Hipster Scale

Dive Bar Rating

Opened in 1947 as a drive-in restaurant called the Hilltop Lounge, and converted in 1959 to a bar because the two friends who built and operated it got sick of customers taking their carhops and marrying them, the Squeeze Inn acquired its current moniker in 1995 when the original owners decided enough was enough—the construction of I-70 had left their tiny tavern, which sits back on a massive parking lot along what's now essentially a frontage road, in the shadow of a monster. And besides: They were old, and the grandkids weren't going to stay young forever.

The maple coolers with chrome latches, black-and-white checkered linoleum floor, brick-wall-mounted turn-page jukebox (64% country, 35% classic rock, 1% Pussycat Dolls)—it's all as original and authentic as the idea that a 400 square-foot bar (capacity: 28) could thrive for more than 60 years in a residential neighborhood. Never in my life have I seen drop ceiling tiles as cigarette-smoke stained as the ones that hover above the Squeeze. These tiles—maintained, I reckon, just as much for the sozzled Sharpie scribbles as for general prosperity—are such a dark golden brown color and so encrusted in formaldehyde and other second-hand chemicals that they actually look like bricks. No shit.

Like any other group of regulars so tight they're more like family than friends, the fine folks who literally squeeze in, on and around the five or so tables, 18 chairs and 8-10 bar stools crave cold beer, stiff drinks, fast motorcycles and classic cars. To wit: The annual, formerly semi-annual, car show held in the parking lot each spring is so popular, there's a permanent tap installed on the side of the bar to facilitate easy access to $2 beers. On bartendress Dawn's last day, a group of guys who arrived on motorcycles hoot, holler and knock over chairs while rolling dice against one another; a man so at home within these cramped confines that he walks around the bar and pours himself a new PBR while Dawn's out smoking has brought his shaggy dog with him—a regular in its own right, the little guy stands on a stool, props his front paws on the bar top and eats ice cubes off a napkin; and an itty-bitty Asian man with a roll-top Igloo cooler walks itty-bitty circles around the room trying to sell homemade egg rolls.

While not afflicted with claustrophobia, I typically try to steer clear of joints so chockablock I could sip from three different drinks at once. For the Squeeze Inn, I'll make an exception every time.

# The Viking

*4888 West Colfax Avenue*
Phone: 303-623-3256 7AM CASH

Hipster Scale

Dive Bar Rating

A warning, via whiteboard, from the staff at the Viking:

YOU NEED TO GET THE HELL OUT OF HERE WHEN:

- You run your big fucking mouth because the bar is out of something
- You call the bartender dirty names in another language, unaware she can translate
- You annoy the other bar customers with your excessive, repetitive, persistent-fucking ear-piercing chatter
- You imply you are the sole provider of this bar's income
- You blame the bartender for loosing (sic) your shit
- You declare your personal issues take priority when we all feel life sucks
- You fight and get pissed off at the bartender for stopping you

WE ARE ALL HERE TO DRINK LET'S TRY TO GET ALONG

Formerly the Tap Inn (Diamond, the bartendress, drank here twenty-odd years ago when it was a 3.2 joint), the cash-only Viking may be a bit harsh, but it's not heartless: Winners of the customer-of-the-week drawing every Sunday snag a free drink every day for a week if they claim it. During Broncos games, touchdown shots are on the house. And you can grab a homemade burrito from the Crock-Pot for just a few bucks.

The current color scheme—purple and orange—is consistent down to the bar stools and the walls in the bathroom (no mirror, no paper towels). Knickknacks, stuffed animals and other crap hold up the wall behind the bar, alongside white wire racks/shelves of chips and snacks. Two frozen-pizza ovens heat up the only other fare available. Beneath a lighted hologram Budweiser sign featuring a wooden duck, shell casings, binoculars, a duck caller and a camouflage hat sits a man selling plastic-wrapped red roses out of a white bucket while scratching lottery tickets.

Part biker bar, part West Colfax roughneck hangout, the Viking will serve anyone who can keep his or her shit together. While I'm smoking on the side patio—which sports planter boxes on the railings, a covered tent in the winter and a grill for summer BBQs—one of the owners swings open the door and, without looking, hawks a loogie right at me. It lands within a pre-pubescent facial hair of my rubber-toed sneaker. "My bad, bro!" he offers. During another break, a paunchy Latina gal with poor balance tells me she had to stay away for a while because she got mixed up in some harder shit. "You're feeling better now, though?" I ask. She, too, spits (though not at me), flicks her butt in the opposite direction of the sand bucket, then screams:

"It's good to be back, baby!"

## Best Burgers

**My Brother's Bar**

**Candlelight Tavern**

**The Cherry Cricket**

**Stockyard Saloon**

**Thunderbird Lounge**

**Gabor's**

# White Horse Bar

*5130 West Alameda Avenue*
*Phone: 303-935-2656 CASH*

Hipster Scale

Dive Bar Rating

"This here's an Indian hangout," Gary reveals to me and three friends after just a few minutes bellied up to the bar he's tending. There are no Native Americans present, which I assume explains how candid white Gary is about the regulars. During the Denver March Pow-Wow, he tells us, the owner brings in 3 bouncers at night just to keep things cool (the bar never employs bouncers otherwise). Most nights, he adds, the White Horse doesn't get busy until around 9 p.m. "That's when all the crazies show up." He's a nice enough guy, Gary with the painful-to-look-at rotten teeth, and it turns out we grew up in the same Illinois town – he and one of my sisters went to the same high school, though he graduated about 30 years (in '68) before she.

Opened in the late '50s, the White Horse hasn't seen much TLC since the current owners bought it in 1974—if ever. The bathroom floors are caving in and patched with duct tape; pieces of rectangular plywood act as toilet lids and come with the message "Hold Handle Down (down arrow) until finish flushing Thank You." If you hold the handle down too far, though, the plywood lifts up and water leaks out. So, you know, watch out for that. An obsolete dance floor in the middle of the room is surrounded by dingy floral carpet, and many of the theme-keeping white horse statues, paintings and plaques are permanently stained yellow.

Like all good dives, the Horse enforces policy via hand-scrawled messages on neon poster board. A few examples: To score a cue ball for one of the three pool tables, you'll have to forfeit an ID; the pay phone costs 50 cents and there's a 3 minute limit ("No Exceptions!"); and, most importantly, "First fight. Last drink. Permanent 86." Toxic orange squares of poster board also find homes atop various liquor bottles, where they advertise "2 for $5.00," "$2.00 :)," and "2-4-1 $5.00 :)" specials. The featured booze—on my visit: Windsor Canadian Whisky, Cactus Juice, Cinnamon Schnapps, Watermelon Pucker, Tuaca and Hornitos—changes every week or whenever the owner feels like it. A jug of Livingston White Zinfandel inexplicably contains red wine.

And while the red/green/yellow twinkle lights strung along the booths and the neon-backlit glass bricks below the bar are wonderful touches, the award for my favorite detail goes to the Coors poster hung on the wood paneling behind the corner stool that shows an apron-clad E.T. wiping up a spotless bar with a rag and the message, "If you go beyond your limit, please don't drive. 'Phone Home.'"

## Best Patios

**Bulldog Bar**

**Charlie Brown's Bar & Grill**

**Club 404**

**Hangar Bar**

**Herb's**

**Lancer Lounge**

**Ogden Street South**

**Park Tavern & Restaurant**

**Rustic Tavern**

**Old Curtis Street Bar**

**Hangar Bar**

# EAST DENVER

## The Dirty Duck Bar
*4780 East Evans Avenue*
*Phone: 303-758-3667*

*Hipster Scale*

*Dive Bar Rating*

Unless I'm with a group of four or more, my preference is always to belly up at the bar. So to say I appreciate a padded bar rail and moveable stools when I find 'em is to express a grave understatement. To wit: More than once in the process of researching this book, I woke up the morning after an eight-hour, five-plus-dive bender with debilitating lower-back pain and bruises near my elbows. And when I say debilitating, I don't mean, "Ow, my back and arms hurt"—I mean heating pads and I.C.E.

The Dirty Duck Bar, a.k.a. the Dirty Bird, has both—elbow pads along the bar ledge and mobile stools. It also stocks more than 50 kinds of liquor; displays almost 25 different available shots on a yellow snowboard by the front door; serves cheap-ass burgers and pizza; and maintains two of the better 24/7 drink specials I've seen: Jagermeister and Bullmeister shots for right around $3 and Budweiser pitchers for $6.50. And the prices have recently gone up.

My last visit to the Duck was at the tail end of one of the aforementioned benders, so shit seems a bit surreal in retrospect. Still, the following anecdotes feel appropriate:

At one point, the huge hi-def above our heads was showing an extended Shark vacuum infomercial and the sound was blaring out the entire PA. My buddy and I must have been cringing, because the bartender wandered over and asked if we liked metal. When I answered, "Depends?" he shook both his arms in excitement, swiveled his neck in a "Git 'er done" sort of way and proceeded to play 20 straight minutes of some seriously gnarly shit on the juke. Talk about cringing.

As the shredding commenced and my brain began to bleed a little, a woman hustled in and ordered a well rum and coke. When the air-guitar-ing tender delivered it, she emptied her pockets onto the bar and paid with nine quarters and five dimes. To her credit, she tipped $.70—in dimes and nickels—before slamming her drink and hustling out.

Just before last call, a dude in coveralls and work boots noticed the Big Buck Hunter game and yelled across the room to his friend, "Hey Red! They got one of them kill-all-the-animals-with-a-gun games!"

Git 'er done.

# Dr. Proctor's Lounge

*4201 East Mississippi Avenue*
*Phone: 303-756-1665*

*Hipster Scale*

*Dive Bar Rating*

In addition to six pool tables, foosball and darts, Dr. Proctor's, a straightforward strip-mall sports dive, also maintains an impressive collection of Denver team memorabilia and throwback Sports Page covers in tacky, Winston-sponsored, gold frames. Wood paneling, a drop ceiling and carpet come standard, and the NASCAR crap is minimal, though a red #9 helmet-turned-lamp hangs at the end of the bar. A strong offering of televisions both big and small (hi-def and tube) broadcast games from open to close, attracting crowd sizes second only to league billiards play and karaoke on Saturday nights.

The crowd is working class through and through—a healthy mix of ages and skin colors, with un-ironic facial hair, shaved heads, neck tattoos and cell phones on hip holsters a la mode. Once while working through a $6 pitcher at one of the main area's high-tops, I watched a feeble creeper in jean shorts and a cut-off tee slink in without buying a drink, play four quarter's worth of erotic photo hunt (boobs, not balls) on the Touch Master 8000 (circa 19996) game console, then slink out. No one else seemed to notice. Not even the waitress, who, sans apron, notepad or tray, diligently worked the room in a hooded sweatshirt and jeans.

Pretty straightforward.

# Hangar Bar

*8001 East Colfax Avenue*
*Phone: 303-320-6683*

Hipster Scale

Dive Bar Rating

It's one thing to belly up. At Hangar Bar, it's another thing entirely. The bolted-down stools are positioned so close to the wooden elbow rest/ledge that extends from the chipped, Formica-surfaced bar that you leave with bruises on your sternum and knees if you settle in for long enough. Which I do happily on Saturday night visits, thanks to live blues bands shaking the walls of this tiny tiki-hut looking tavern from a makeshift stage—and an incredible bar staff that keeps my pints full when I finish them and my ego in check when I'm so drunk I spill them.

Born in 1938—the same year as the nearby Lowry Air Force Base —the Hangar Bar specialized in stiff drinks and Colorado camaraderie for Air Force pilots and crew until 1994, when the base closed. Owners changed over the years, as did the clientele, but today the Hangar remains a no-nonsense dive serving up the same stiff drinks and open-arms attitude. Aeronautically themed down to the U.S. Army Air Corp posters and airplane models resting on the microwave behind the bar, the crowning jewel is the Beer Can Bomber, an airplane sculpture suspended from the ceiling that's roughly the size of a MINI Cooper. Comprised of more than 300 vintage beer cans, the Bomber appears to repeat cans in only one case—with a handful of identical Coors cans that serve as propellers. (Two modern Bud bottles, however, stand in for missiles.)

When the black-and-orange-checkered floors are shakin' beneath the weight of hot blues and heavy dancing, the only seats to be had at the Hangar are at the bar. Every other night, a few high tops surround the two pool tables and an L-shaped booth sits where the band plays. Year-round, though, there's a fenced-in outdoor patio past the bathrooms and cigarette machine with plenty of room for smokers and fresh-air seekers to take a load off. Happy hours are 4-7 p.m. and 10 p.m.-midnight Monday-Friday, though there's always a $2.50 drink special going on (just ask if it's not obvious). With a rotating schedule of special events and pricing—colleges nights, ladies nights, man appreciation nights, karaoke nights and entire days of free pool—there's a always a reason to trek east down Colfax and into the Hangar.

The Beer Can Bomber alone is reason to land here.

4958 East Colfax Avenue
Phone: 303-320-9337

Hipster Scale

Dive Bar Rating

Heard the one about the straight guy and the gay bar?

Guy walks into a bar alone, pulls up a stool and is greeted by the bartender, who introduces himself as Dan. Dan asks for an ID, holds out his hand for a courtesy shake and says, "Nice to meet you. Haven't seen you before; first time?" Yes. Dan introduces Guy to the three men in their late thirties/early forties chatting at the end of the bar. "Hey, everyone," Dan says. "This is Drew." Two come over for courtesy shakes, then return to their spots. Guy thinks, "Everyone here is so friendly."

Guy peels the label back on his cold beer (bottles and cans only) and wipes the sweat from his brow with his wrist. He notices a plethora of touch-screen game consoles, a dartboard in the back, a slew of unoccupied tall tables. He and Dan make small talk. "You live in the neighborhood?" Dan asks. "Nah," Guy responds, "but I like the area. Been across the street at the Elm before, but this is more my kind of place—cool, quiet, dark." Dan smiles. "This your bar?" Guy asks Dan. No, but he's been around forever, Dan explains while sipping from a bottle of Tecate Light. "Used to work here back in '86, when it switched over from a straight biker bar to the R&R." Somewhere inside Guy's head, a flashbulb explodes; a kitchen timer set to ten minutes goes ping! Guy thinks, "Ohhhhhh...," pulls the last sip of beer from his bottle and excuses himself for a cigarette.

Outside, Guy calls his closest gay friend. "You'll never guess what I just did," he says. "I've been inside the R&R for a solid ten minutes and had no idea it was a gay bar." Friend is confused: "Wait, where are you?" R&R (or R-R) Denver. "Here's the best part," Guy continues. "At one point, I told the bartender that I'd been to a bar across the street, but that this was more my kind of place—cool, quiet, dark." Friend laughs through the phone and onto the sidewalk. "Good luck with that," he closes.

On his way back inside, Guy notices everything he failed to before—the rainbow-colored squares painted on the wooden door; the issues of gayzette and PINK just inside the entrance; the tiny, multi-colored mirror ball positioned at beer-bottle-option level behind the bar. Oh, and all the men. "What a fuckin' idiot I am," Guy thinks. Then he orders another beer—a Landshark island-style lager, from the man behind Margaritaville—and asks Dan about the Buck a Chance jar above the beer tubs. Dan tells him that a dollar purchases a paper token with a unique number on it. The purchaser's name and token number are recorded in a small three-ring notebook, and every time the purchaser comes in, he or she can pay another dollar to "activate" the number. Then, at the end of every night, the on-duty tender pulls a token, and if the number has been activated the same day, that person wins the pot. The odds seem low—Guy's number is well over 550—but he purchases and activates anyway.

Gay or straight, Guy knows a great dive when he sees one.

# Ram Lounge

*5026 East Colfax Avenue*
*Phone: 303-394-4156 7AM CASH*

Hipster Scale

Dive Bar Rating

If I've learned anything about dive bars in the process of visiting more than 100 of them, it's that they don't scare me. I'm not afraid to walk into anywhere, even alone. Even if there are no windows, it's late at night and I end up being the only honky or gringo. This is not to say I'll never be the victim of random crime or singled out unfairly in a bar where I'm just plain unwelcome, but I've learned that the best way to avoid getting jumped, stabbed or worse is to not ask for it—I keep my mouth shut when necessary, tip well whenever possible and concentrate on my drink

The Ram Lounge, easily one of East Colfax's roughest, is the kind of place where a good incarceration story is always in progress; where homeless and various other transient folk can afford to snag a drink without being hustled out for fear of upsetting the expensive set; where the ethnic minority is often Caucasian; or where you're just as likely to be hit up for drugs as the dude who's actually selling. In other words, it's exactly the kind of place most white people are afraid of.

My friend Neddy absolutely loves this place. He's an average white guy with limited funds and a healthier-than-average appetite for cheap domestic beer, so 7 a.m. happy hour, Busch on tap, $6.50 pitchers and a leave-no-trace cash-only policy greatly appeal to him. Free shots of peach brandy every time the Broncos score, even if they do taste like perfume, are also enticing, as is a Sunday spread of free food (turkey, rolls, chili, tacos, etc.) And though Neddy loves him some metal and psychedelia, a jukebox full of soul jams and disco hits always puts him in the mood to drink (and occasionally get hit on by 50 year-old black women).

If embarrassingly bad paintings—one depicts a naked white woman with small hips but hugely disproportionate thighs—a sparkle ceiling and guys flossing their teeth at the bar don't entice you, there's a makeshift patio in the alley by the Dumpster, complete with mismatched chairs, a beat-up orange couch and a torn umbrella.

All together now: I am not afraid. I am not afraid.

DENVER'S BEST DIVE BARS

# Retreat Lounge

*2186 South Colorado Boulevard*
*Phone: 303-756-1869*

Hipster Scale

Dive Bar Rating

Not to be confused with The Retreat—the on-premise swingers club for couples and single females located west of downtown Denver—the Retreat Lounge occupies a buried slice of strip mall hell completely hidden from Colorado Boulevard. Inside, the two spacious rooms couldn't be more different from one another. To the left is a cozy-if-not-cramped main bar area (with a padded ledge—score!), a massive projection screen that shows sporting events and facilitates collaborative video gaming (think Wii Sports) and a whole mess of tables and odd vinyl office chairs for relaxing or eating off the modest bar menu. To the right is a veritable alternate universe. Either that or I'm always too drunk when I visit.

In reality, the other room is for overflow and recreation—a free shuffleboard table, a wacky UltraPin digital (!) pinball machine, questionably functioning tube televisions and another mess of awkwardly upholstered, black vinyl chairs run amok. Oh, and a set of newish-looking boombox speakers mounted next to obsolete, dust-encrusted speakers. Which is strange, but whatever.

A friend and I once stumbled in after a long night of bellying up and binging, and we immediately made friends with a woman named Kim and her friend Michael, who insisted we call him Michelangelo and handed us both laminated color cards for his handyman/remodeling business (with his actual name on them). The whole game room smelled faintly of natural gas, but we pushed on, playing a couple games of shuffleboard together, smoking out front, and generally acting stupid. This is just how the Retreat rolls—friendly, inviting, a little bit bizarre.

The Mile High Brown Backers have been calling the Retreat Lounge home base since 1993—tailgating in the parking lot before the bar opens on Sunday mornings and cramming around every table to eat and drink. I'm also told that Sunday nights are for movies, and that regulars are chosen to run to the video store and bring back whatever they fancy. Which is awesome.

And way better than awkward group sex with a bunch of strangers.

# Sam's Bar & Lounge

*6801 Leetsdale Drive*
*Phone: 303-322-6401*

Sam's Bar & Lounge is one of those rare dives you just feel really good walking into—bright walls, plenty of natural light, warm wood tones, linoleum/tile floor. It's cut from a quality, 1950s, still-glowing-neon-sign mold, and both operated and inhabited by the type of folks who would take offense if you referred to it as a hole in the wall. As any seasoned barfly knows, there's a huge difference between run-down, as which many dives in this collection qualify, and just old, which describes Sam's. Yeah, the bathroom door doesn't lock, the bar of soap is a bit limey and a coin-operated vending machine dispenses cardboard nudie photos. So? After 55 years, at least there's a door. And soap. And who's going to complain about boobs? Even gay men love breasts. I'm serious.

Attracting everyone from working-class stiffs to retired veterans to happy-hour-seeking suits to neck-tattoo tough guys, Sam's not only serves cheap cold ones and cocktails, but also an impressive red-basket-and-wax-paper menu of wings, fries, burgers, sandwiches and Mexican food—all of it under $10. On Sundays, the Hangover Special from 9 a.m. until noon includes a Bloody Mary and a bowl of "famous" green chili for $7.50. Kids aren't allowed after 3 p.m., but that still leaves 8 hours to strap in the car seats and get a solid daylight buzz going while the little ones play pool, throw darts or shake the Shadow-themed pinball machine. Maybe a babysitter is a better idea, but you do what you want—it's your therapy bill later on.

When I visited during the heart of 2009's NCAA basketball tourney, four of the five televisions—one flatscreen, one giant rear-projection and three simple tubes—were turned to NASCAR instead of hoops. Autographed and decorated dollar bills hung from the ceiling over the rectangular bar; and a stuffed Tasmanian Devil doll was nailed to the wall above the register with a $5 bill tacked to its mouth. This sort of eclectic décor, de rigueur in the dive-bar world, is a comforting reminder of why dives like Sam's feel so good to walk into.

# Thunderbird Lounge

721 Quebec Street
Phone: 303-377-5730

Hipster Scale

Dive Bar Rating

Something about the (Harvey) Thunderbird Lounge makes me want to take off my shoes and get more comfortable, maybe hang my coat in the hallway closet and then grab a bite from the fridge—for walking into the warmly lit, thinly carpeted dive feels a lot like coming home for the holidays, like arriving late to a party where everyone knows my name.

It helps that my friends Carey and Joe are longtime regulars, and that when we arrive, we walk straight to a group of tall tables and booths on the restaurant side of the bar (known as the Spitfire), where three generations of families are already in full Friday-night swing. Steak knives and pinkish puddles of meat grease—evidence of tonight's prime-rib special—lie abandoned on porcelain plates and tabletops as the parents and grandparents who left them there drink draft beer and wine, tell stories and smile. Their elementary-age kin catapult Lord of the Rings action figures over fake poinsettia displays in brown wicker pots, sip soda from plastic cups with lids, and eat popcorn chicken and onion rings out of red plastic baskets lined with checkered waxed paper. Everyone seems happy to be here, and by God, so are we.

Over on the T-Bird side, it's more of the same. Twenty-somethings crowded into a pink padded booth share pitchers of beer and baskets of frings while paying haphazard attention to the corner-mounted TVs and making plans for the rest of the night. Three women in pink and black embroidered bowling shirts that read "Dolls With Balls" laugh like sisters and take shots of something chilled. And in the blue-painted, concrete-walled pool room, a couple of boys roll the cue ball back and forth and rub chalk between their fingers. But they're on borrowed time: No kids on the pool tables after 8 p.m.—bar policy.

On both sides of the bar, flatscreen TVs and an Internet jukebox share real estate with glossies of long-retired stock cars, Broncos and Buffs memorabilia, Budweiser mirrors commemorating fifty years of NASCAR, and black-and-white pictures of Union Station and downtown Denver at the turn of the last century. Trophies and team pictures from Thunderbird-sponsored golf tournaments and championship bar-league billiards teams litter the walls and dark, dusty corners. Computer-printed signs hung with worn-out invisible tape advertise Sunday brunch (Bloody Mary bar!) in bold red letters.

While I drink a bottle of Bud and take everything in, Carey cradles her six-month-old baby, calls the waitresses (Sandy and Kelly) by name, orders special items from the kitchen that aren't on the menu. Joe's son Alex orders "the usual," and Sandy knows what he means. When our food comes, we pass plates like family. When it's gone, we loosen our belts and rub our bellies; we clean up after ourselves and compliment the cook like Ma made it herself.

It's Friday-night family time, and we might as well be at home.

## Darts

**BJ's Carousel**

**Candlelight Tavern**

**Carioca Café (Bar Bar)**

**Dr. Proctor's Lounge**

**R&R Denver**

**Sam's Bar & Lounge**

**William's Tavern**

**Ease On In Lounge**

# NORTH DENVER

# Arabian Bar

*3360 Navajo Street*
*Phone: 303-433-0151 CASH*

Hipster Scale

Dive Bar Rating

So the urinals are leaky and loose, (barely) attached to the wall with the help of a two-by-four; so the light hanging over the side-door steps where smokers gather flickers in seizure-inducing fits; so the back half of this tiny tavern has, on occasion, smelled like a mildew-soaked mop. So what? When the overhead is low, everybody wins.

By the time I walk through the doors of the Arabian Bar around 8:30 p.m., a healthy Monday-night crowd is shooting pool, fiddling with the classic jukebox and punching buttons on the Wild Double Up poker machine. I belly up next to a guy salting a fried-chicken-and-mashed-potatoes microwave dinner with a Peppermint Schnapps shooter-turned-shaker and reading a coverless paperback.

The bartendress, a sweet, talkative young woman who has tended bar at the Arabian for three years because her grandfather used to be a regular, brings me a Bud bottle before doing a shot of Cuervo with a customer. The owners—a couple in their seventies—aren't in tonight. On previous visits, they've affectionately (though sternly) corrected my billiards shot, fed me dollars from the register for the juke—three songs for a dollar: Dwight Yoakam, Buck Owens, Ray Charles—and invited me back for a complimentary Thanksgiving dinner with all the fixins. Too bad: Their company alone is worth the trip.

There are no mysteries to the Arabian's dirt-cheap, cash-only pricing scheme—domestic bottles are always $2 and $1.75 during happy hour (there's no draft beer), and the dozen or so handles of liquor on the counter behind the bar have laughably low prices written right on them in black Sharpie. Way back when the Coors Tavern was still across the street (it's now the remodeled-around-the-edges Highland Tavern) regulars over there would shuffle over between drinks, take shots (the Arabian was always cheaper) and shuffle back. These days, the young, hip and clever are known to finish their shifts at various neighborhood bars and restaurants and eschew the Highland's bright lights and pricey microbrews for quiet conversation in the Arabian's orange vinyl booths. They choose dollar bills tacked to the ceiling and a rustically cool "Wire of the Old West" display over the chance of seeing or being seen. I certainly don't blame them.

# Ease On In Lounge

*4058 Fox Street*
*Phone: 303-458-8091*

*Hipster Scale*

*Dive Bar Rating*

Madeline is rolling her eyes. Louie, a squinty, hunched-over octogenarian with a rubber-bottomed cane, has just shuffled into the Ease On In Lounge for the second time today. He wants to see the Nuggets pool again to make sure he hasn't won. "I already told ya, Lou," Madeline says impatiently from behind the bar. "You didn't win." He still checks every square. Again. Then he shuffles out.

Once Louie's gone, Madeline turns her attention back to the handful of regulars eating free tacos and fruit from the corner spread and gossiping about who's "running around" with whom, who's died recently, who owes who money and who's in jail. As it turns out, a fellow bartender's been in the clank and doesn't get out for another 10 days, which explains why Madeline's been working extra shifts all week. On the upside, she won a Rockies pool recently, netting her $125. When, from down the bar, Joe razzes her for rigging the numbers, she whips her towel at him and fires, "Don't start no shit, Joe."

As the regs continue to munch on hard shells and cantaloupe, and another older gentleman (also with a cane) struggles to keep his drowsy eyes out of his draft beer, a young man with unkempt facial hair and a pony tail wanders in with Nuggets T-shirts on hangers. "Fifteen bucks or two for $25," he tells us. "All sizes; good-quality cotton." No one bites. Not on the shirts, at least.

On Friday and Saturday nights, Latino rock band Remedy fills the floor and shakes the frame from a corner stage outfitted in a floor-to-ceiling backdrop of green and blue tinsel. Southwestern-colored carpet is stapled to almost every other wall. For a good 10 minutes of my visit, another employee vacuums the surface of the lone pool table while cleaning each of the balls. I grab a smoke on the spacious side patio to dodge the noise, then a piss in the surprisingly clean bathroom (the fake plants and bad art make up for the sanitary faux pas). When I return, I notice a cheap scrolling marquee advertising $3 pitchers on Mondays and free, hangover-curing menudo on Sundays until it's gone.

Free tacos, fruit and soup; live music on weekends; good gossip—I wouldn't ask for anything more. Except another drink, of course.

# The Grizzly Rose

*5450 North Valley Highway*
*Phone: 303-295-1330*

*Hipster Scale*  *Dive Bar Rating*

The trick to making any mechanical bull your bitch is to choke up on the saddle with your knees and thighs tight against the frame, lean loosely over the rope so that your center of gravity points toward the sky when it bucks, and hold on with one hand while waving your free arm (in slap-that-ass motions) for balance. Then again, I'm wearing New Balances and a hooded sweatshirt, have toppled eight or nine MGD longnecks in just under two hours, and don't know shit about shit (I've never done this before). It shows: Though I bounce and sway for a few moderate twists and turns, I'm eventually reduced to gripping the rope with both hands and then tumbling to the air-cushioned floor like a small child being tossed from a teeter-totter.

A 40,000-square-foot saloon and dance hall with an incredible, 5,000-square-foot floating hardwood dance floor and massive live-music stage, the Grizzly Rose is one of America's last true honky tonks. Though it is as authentic as a weathered ranch hand brandishing a cattle prod and a week's worth of Western Slope dirt underneath his fingernails, at times I feel like I'm lost in the Western section of a Six Flags theme park. Maybe it's the matching wooden signs for "Outhouses" (cowboys to the left, cowgirls to the right), "Grub" (the Chuck Wagon Grill), the "Shine Parlor" (where dozens of signed glossies of everyone from John Michael Montgomery to Bucky Covington personally thank Nancy for the $5 shine) and "General Store." Maybe it's the large glass display cases featuring mannequins in Grizzly garb posing in desert landscapes, the arcade games and Toy Box machine offering chances at stuffed animals for fifty cents, the recessed, covered alleys all along the outer edge. Probably, though, it's simply the Grizzly's size.

To truly get a feel for the average clientele, imagine loading a ship full of pickup-drivin', square-dancin' country-Western fans, sailing it across a sea of cowboy hats and steel-tipped boots and crashing it onto the rocks of tapered, creased-down-the-middle Wrangler blue jeans. Imagine employees in Confederate-flag tank tops slinging

$3 bottles from beer tubs and security guards with gigantic belt buckles and jangly keys policing the sweaty, drunken masses like sheriffs from the Wild West. Black cowboys? You can find one if you look long enough. Latinos? Plenty.

I don't mind country music and line dancing, though neither are my favorite, so when I'm not watching tie-down roping or poker on the flatscreens, I escape into the Tobacco Shop, a well-ventilated, closed-door area where I can both purchase and partake in my addiction. On one such visit (the band's on a break and the speakers in the main room are blaring Confederate Railroad's "Trashy Women"), I chat with a bald gentleman named Dan who couldn't be more pleased with the way his boots look after a quick shine; on another, I watch a young woman in a tattered recliner fall asleep with a lit cigarette resting on her left leg. When she finally wakes and leaves, a guard follows close behind to ensure that she makes for the exit instead of another drink. (Security doesn't always have such little fires to piss on. The December 2008 shooting death of guard Timothy Minnick—the result of a parking-lot altercation between security and three men wearing hooded sweatshirts and bandannas over their faces—is proof that the Grizzly is not, in fact, a theme park, and that the West can still be wild.)

The Grizzly is famous for live music six nights a week and its mechanical bull (which you can ride until you pass out for a cool $20), but roping contests (you can bring your own), Texas Hold 'Em tournaments (when you can also drink unlimited draft beer for $7) and dance lessons (everything from line to swing to two-step) keep the place teeming with folks who'd rather shoot themselves in the feet than set foot inside Coyote Ugly or Cowboy Lounge.

# JD's Neighborhood Bar

*2001 West 48th Avenue*　　　　*Hipster Scale*　　*Dive Bar Rating*
*Phone: 303-433-2050*

When the It'll Do Lounge closed its doors in 2006 after 27 years in business, regulars wondered what would happen to the small structure at 2001 West 48th Avenue. A little more than a year later, JD's Neighborhood Bar happened, and if Deb the bartendress's word is as good as her Bloody Marys, business has been booming. Longtime fans of the It'll Do will notice a new coat of green paint and more than a few new faces, but much is still the same.

Dozing old men are a well-worn tavern cliché. On my first visit to JD's, two Depression-era gentlemen silently nursing Budweiser draws at the end of the bar do nothing to break the stereotype. They are quite possibly the hoariest, most adorable old fellows I have ever seen slumped over. They speak slowly, drink slowly and hobble to the bathroom slowly. They also flirt: One of them refers to Deb as the "cutie on duty" and pulls her in for an awkward side hug and kiss on the cheek when he leaves.

Next to the full-size Colorado Lottery scratch-ticket machine, the Internet juke plays everything from Dolly Parton and Kenny Rogers to Tejano songs that the predominately Latino crowd carols along to. A countertop menu offers nachos, breakfast burritos and pizza slices for a few bucks apiece, though free, fresh popcorn is made to order, and a snack/cigarette machine by the door to the smoking patio displays a smattering of cheap snacks and packs of cancer sticks.

In between the liquor bottles on the back counter and a banner advertising $2 Jell-O shots sits a plastic tub labeled "Cherry Bombs: 4 for $1." Inside, actual cherries soak up Bacardi 151 and well vodka. I recommend skipping the gimmick and ordering up one of bartendress Deb's mean Bloody Marys. If things get out of hand, night shift muscle dressed in oversized black tees and security-camera footage fed to closed circuit TVs should keep you in your stool well past It'll Do and straight into Done.

# Mr. A's Restaurant & Lounge

*3200 East 40th Avenue*                    *Hipster Scale*          *Dive Bar Rating*
Phone: 303-322-9005

Before entering the self-ascribed "friendliest lounge" in all of Denver, the sign just outside the front door announcing the bar's dress code might give you pause: After 8 p.m., it warns, no "do" rags, stocking caps, backward caps, "colors," baggy pants, athletic gear, sweats or shirtless sleeves. Basically: No tough-guy gang-mentality crap inside. If that's your deal, fine, but it ain't gonna fly here.

Which is fitting, because while plenty of white folk wouldn't set foot inside a dark dive frequented by African-American regulars for fear of being shivved, Mr. A's really does live up to its motto. Like a fathead on a mission for self-inflicted financial ruin, I once drank three-quarters of a 16-ounce Budweiser bottle before a sweet woman in church clothes came in to tell me I'd left my keys dangling from the ignition of my scooter in the parking lot. On another occasion, I spent the length of two cigarettes on the generous side patio —complete with mismatched chairs and a ramshackle gazebo filled with picnic tables—shooting the breeze with an affable guy named Charles, a.k.a. D.J. Chazz, who spins smooth jazz, R&B, old-school and rap on Saturdays. And while I've never been invited to join the six old dudes playing dominoes at the back table, I have happily helped myself to the spreads of free food in foil containers.

With a small stage surrounded by railings, plenty of mirrors with gaudy gold detail and a jukebox specializing in jazz instrumentals, classic soul and a smattering of funk, I always half expect fly ladies to emerge and remove their tops at any moment. On the wall next to a broken tabletop Pac Man machine hang 20 or so photos of the Ebony Maniacs Hot Rod Club; in the entryway hang a 2004 NFL schedule and photographs of smiling regulars; and at the bar hang a faithful flock of patrons whose drinks are poured before they can even sit down.

# Phil's Place

*3463 Larimer Street   7AM*
Phone: 303-298-1559

*Hipster Scale*

*Dive Bar Rating*

Though Phil Garcia and his classic dive at 3463 Larimer—a bar formerly known as Our Place, which he purchased in 2002—are technically a few years shy of the ten-years-or-more-of-history policy that guided the selection of joints featured in these pages, the family history he brought with him when he moved into the building more than makes up for it. Phil's great uncle, J.R. Perez, owned and operated the Bamboo Hut (a gone-but-not-forgotten hole in the wall once located a mile south on Larimer), and his great aunts and grandmother all had a hand in the Mexico City Lounge. Junie, Phil's mother, was there for all of it, cooking enchiladas and burritos and some of Denver's better-regarded green chile from peppers grown on the family farm in Commerce City. And since 2004, she's been running Junie's Kitchen in the back of her son's Place—serving the same great fare, now exclusively in takeout containers.

That doesn't mean you shouldn't pull up a green-padded chair at one of the six tables covered in plastic blue-and-white-checkered tablecloths. Better yet, grab a stool at the bar (if you can find one) and let one of the Garcias serve you a $2 Coors or a double-tall mixed drink. If game shows are on, be prepared to talk some serious shit at the TVs with the others. "My God!" they'll scream at clueless contestants. "The answer ain't 90, bitch!" they'll shriek in disbelief. They mean well. Kind of.

Handwritten signs scattered about the green-carpeted room silently enforce the house rules: "No tabs—only when Phil's here"; "NO kids on Pool Table"; "Any pool ball knocked off the table!!! $1 in the JukeBox." Broncos logos and loyalty appear everywhere—on hand-painted mirrors (not to mention a giant mural on the northeastern-facing outer wall), banners, pennants, bobble heads and pompoms—even on little plastic helmets and jersey cozies covering the beer bottles on the selection shelf behind the bar.

Past the bathrooms and the kitchen, a small outdoor patio offers plastic chairs and a curious accoutrement or two. But inside with the (mostly Latino) regulars is where it's really at. Come early and often. If you don't, you just might find that Phil has closed up early. And you don't want to miss the family.

## Ron & Dan's Keg

*1851 West 38th Avenue*
*Phone: 303-455-9336  CASH*

Hipster Scale     Dive Bar Rating

Ron & Dan's Keg is a simple-as-it-gets biker bar that caters predominantly to a Latino crowd. From open to close, two, ten, sometimes twenty or more motorcycles are scattered throughout the parking lot and around the front door. A sign on the outside of the bar warns, simply, "No Kids"; a sign on the inside, just above the door, reads, "First Fight Last Drink. This Is A Bar Not A Drug Store." So if you've got your kids tonight, have beef that needs settling with one of the Los Bravos or have little plastic Baggies in your pocket that need to be unloaded, you really oughta find somewhere else to unwind. Especially since, if you're looking to trade blows or product for cash, taking it outside won't work to your advantage: Two displays at both ends of the bar project nine different security views of the parking lot and surrounding area. That shit is on lockdown, sucka.

Two pool tables, a bevy of white resin chairs surrounding wood tables and a handful of high tops make up the whole layout. Above the long bar, which serves pitchers at the price of mixed drinks and enough flavors of Pucker to take different-colored shots all night, hang 28 old-school NFL team mirrors—old enough to include the Houston Oilers and less than 32 teams. Most surprising about the décor, however, is the intricately carved and lacquered woodwork along the ceiling, bar, mirrors and door frames. If it weren't for the lawn furniture around the pool tables, you might think you were in an Amish furniture store instead of a biker bar. But, no: One glance at the vending machine stocked with smokes, snacks, pain meds and condoms would remind you exactly where you are.

A simple-as-it-gets biker bar with incredible woodwork.

# Scoreboard Restaurant & Lounge

*3940 York Street*
*Phone: 303-293-9232*

*Hipster Scale*

*Dive Bar Rating*

I have never before asked a bartender for permission to buy a drink. Why would I? Bars, taverns, saloons—they exist for the sole purpose of selling alcohol. Yet my first few seconds inside Scoreboard Restaurant & Lounge are so straight out of a movie—that scene where three white guys walk into a loud bar inhabited solely by black folks, and everybody stops what they're doing to stare (record-scratch sound effect optional)—that my principal instinct is to make sure I'm welcome. "Can we get a drink?" I ask the bartendress. "I don't see why not!" is her almost indignant reply. So we settle in, bellies up, bottles of Bud and Bud Light in hand.

Silvia's been behind the bar since the Scoreboard took over this space twelve years ago. She explains that some nights the crowd starts at Marion's and Mr. A's (down the street and around the corner) and sometimes it starts here. She scoffs at how quickly I drink my beers; she says, "We got some serious drinkers who come in here." She doesn't mean me.

When it's slow, Silvia sits at the end of the bar with us and reminisces about the heyday of Five Points—people everywhere, falling in the streets; the lights and the noise and the way she just knew it was the place to be. She also complains about the light rail D line ruining everything on Welton Street, and dishes about her favorite fried chicken and soul food.

The kitchen at the Scoreboard serves chicken, pork chops, catfish and hot links from open to close. A DJ (tonight just a guy in the back with an overflowing case of compact discs) spins on weekends, karaoke draws a rabble on Tuesday nights, and a dusty old jukebox packed with R&B and soul classics handles the vibe every other night. Long, though not especially narrow, the space is arranged much like a VFW or American Legion hall—a few four-tops toward the front and a low-rise in the back, but mostly rectangular tables with metal-framed padded chairs set up on both sides, cafeteria style. The liquor selection is immense, with an entire section devoted to wells, frou-frou flavors and obscure liqueurs available for $3 a shot.

As the crowd picks up and the rooms makes like it's about to go off, Silvia's seat is occupied by Willy, the owner. He drinks Crown, neat, from a large shot glass and dishes about his days as a union rep. He speaks with an almost melodic cadence, his tales salted liberally with one-liners and offbeat jokes. When he's concentrating, his eyes are closed; when he finds something especially funny, he leans way back in his chair, sticks out his tongue and slaps his left leg repeatedly.

Willy's bread and butter is black, but he's not picky: "I don't care whetha ya tall, short, fat, skinny, black, white, gray or green," he says while staring at his own eyelids, "so long as ya got money to help me pay the mortgage, you're welcome here!" He invites us to a free lunch the next afternoon: Bring three canned goods and eat pig's ears, pig's feet and chili for free. When we finally decide to bail, he shakes our hands and says goodnight. As we slide through the crowd and head into the cold—past a Bud Light banner announcing management's right to search for weapons—we still feel like three white guys leaving an all-black bar, but at least we now feel welcome.

"Be good, y'all," we hear Willy holler at our backs. "And don't stay gone for so long!"

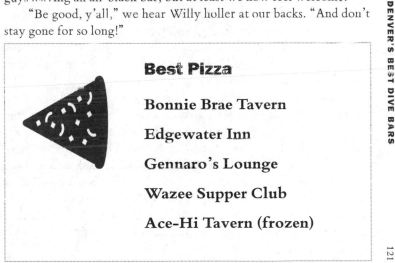

## Best Pizza

**Bonnie Brae Tavern**

**Edgewater Inn**

**Gennaro's Lounge**

**Wazee Supper Club**

**Ace-Hi Tavern (frozen)**

## Sidewinder Tavern

4485 Logan Street
Phone: 303-295-1105

Hipster Scale

Dive Bar Rating

Originally settled in the late 1880s by Slavic immigrants working at the Globe Smelting and Refining Company, the Globeville neighborhood, now primarily Spanish-speaking, has always been isolated —initially by railroad tracks and eventually by the construction of Interstates 25 and 70. How many Denver natives don't even know this hood even really exists, or that a handful of businesses continue to hold on along East 45th Avenue, just southwest of the Washington Street exit on I-70? My guess is most.

One such business, a cozy little dive reminiscent of the Rosa Mia, is the Sidewinder, formerly the Logan Street Grill. According to the proprietor/bartendress, the joint's been around "forever," which probably means since the 1950s or '60s. Like the Rosa, the Sidewinder has a Double Up poker machine, a no-cussing policy, a limited booze selection and a loyal group of regulars who live in the surrounding neighborhood. Unlike the Rosa, a turn-page jukebox is still alive and pumping out country, oldies and soul tunes, and a modest kitchen will kick out nachos, hot Polish sausage and hot dogs. Customers regularly roll dice ($1 = two rolls) in the hopes of hitting Yahtzee (progressive pot) or 4 of a kind (free drink). They also buy each other rounds— even when the recipients aren't present. In these cases, neon-colored plastic shot glasses are set aside as stand-ins for wooden nickels, and the lucky soon-to-be-drunk's name and gift are tallied on the back of an envelope behind the bar.

Though the television situation isn't stellar (two small tube TVs, one large rear-projection screen), it could be a lot worse. In fact, the Sidewinder is a great place to black out while the home team is playing. During Rockies games, for example, Bud Light drafts (the only tap) are $1.50, buckets of Coors Light just $11.25 and shots free if the Rox win. The whole sports scene here may be more subdued than you're used to—hell, they don't even bother turning on the lights during the day unless it's cloudy—but that just means less distractions. From the game. From your drink. From your life.

# Stockyard Saloon

*4710 National Western Drive*
*Phone: 303-298-0525 CASH*

*Hipster Scale*   *Dive Bar Rating*

Some time around the turn of the last century, the building that now houses the Stockyard Saloon was constructed and served as the freight office for the Chicago, Burlington & Quincy Railroad. Livestock was shipped here to be weighed, watered, fed and sold through livestock-commissioned companies headquartered in other parts of the building. When truck freight took over post World War 2, however, packing plants moved to Greeley, Fort Collins and elsewhere to follow auction rings. Which means these days, barring the presence of 500,000-plus spectators and stockmen flooding the next-door National Western Stock Show every January, this once-booming area between the Globeville and Elyria Swansea neighborhoods feels more like an empty industrial wasteland than the inspiration for Denver's lingering rep as a cow town.

Still, the Stockyard Saloon, which dates back 80 or more years and has offered liquid relief under a number of variations on the current name—including the Old West Tavern, the Stockyards Inn Grill & Tap House and simply the Stockyards Inn—continues to hold down the fort, albeit with significantly scaled back hours (weekdays 11 a.m.-8 p.m.) and the absence of a credit card terminal. (The ruined economy means cash only, friends). So while you won't find live music and weekend debauchery inside this second-floor saloon anymore, you will find a solid menu, a loyal lunch and happy-hour crowd and the same wooden bar and expansive back bar shipped across the heartland from one of Al Capone's Chicago joints—a bar complete with hidden compartments and an accompanying Diebold Safe & Lock Co. walk-in safe (currently used for storage).

On my last visit, I sat with a gentleman in rawhide boots and Dickies who called the Stockyard Saloon "one of Denver's best-kept secrets." I nodded in agreement, though I never promised to keep it.

Spread the word.

# Welcome Inn

*3759 Chestnut Place*
*Phone:303-296-7229 7AM CASH*

Hipster Scale

Dive Bar Rating

One of my favorite days off on record begins with a dirt-cheap hot ham and cheese at the Butcher Block Café and a $2 frosty mug of Bud down the street at the Welcome Inn. The joint is empty save a bearded guy with a milk crate of personal belongings doing crossword puzzles in the corner. A frazzled, heavyset bartendress with unkempt hair is on the cordless phone, pacing the length of the bar back and recounting with foul-mouthed enthusiasm a story that she repeats to me in full detail ten minutes later. A story that goes like this: She and her husband own a two-bedroom rental property in Green Valley Ranch, right? And the motherfuckin' low-life tenants of this property haven't paid rent in two months, right? So they go over there last night to confront these sons of bitches and are told that homies are about to roll up with motherfuckin' shotguns to bust caps in both their asses if they don't leave. Heated phrases are exchanged, and the tenants begin shooting firecrackers at them from across the street. So the bartender and her husband call the police; meanwhile, one of the tenants starts burning little bags of drugs in a driveway garbage can. When the cops arrive and ask that tenant for her ID, she fakes like she's going in the house to get it, then hops in her car and speeds away, prompting a high-speed police chase.

"I should probably just sell the place so I don't have to deal with this shit anymore," the bartender says to me when the story is finished. Yeah. Probably.

Four mugs and less than an hour later, I'm busy demolishing high scores on the Megatouch video screen next to me—dutifully typing D-R-E-W into high score after high score on the sparsely populated ranking pages—and half-watching Double Impact on the corner TV, when the bartender's two kids walk in, plop down at the bar and ask for Cokes. The little guy can't be more than seven; he eats chicken nuggets. The girl is maybe seventeen and argues with her ma about doing laundry. They both make easy conversation with the two regulars now seated at the bar and treat the place like a second home, grabbing bags of Doritos and beef jerky from the swivel-tree stand next to the Jager machine. Two guys in phone-company work shirts come to tear the payphone from the wall, and a Coors rep shows up with more banners and cardboard Broncos-schedule displays to add to the already claustrophobic decor of NASCAR clutter and ten-year-old softball trophies. Jean-Claude Van Damme is having soft-core sex on a fishing boat and I'm already half-cut, so I decide to leave. "Be safe, honey," the bartender calls to me. "See you soon," I respond before walking into the buzz-intensifying sunlight.

In this case, "soon" means four hours later, when my buzz has worn off and I return for happy hour. The kids are gone, but the bartender remains. "You're still here?" I ask her. "Back already?" she retorts. I grab the same stool, order a 34-ounce Frozen Belly Buster of Bud (the bar's pride and joy, always $3.50) and go back to shattering records on the Megatouch, this time half-watching the Rockies lead the Brewers in the top of the ninth. I'm halfway through my Belly Buster and pondering a game of pinball when the daughter strolls back in. She gives me the same "You're still here?" look I gave her mother seventeen ounces ago and heads down the bar to talk with her mom, who's throwing dice with a customer. The girl stays only a minute or two; as she leaves, she pats me on the arm and says, "Well, goodbye, whateveryournameis."

It's Drew, I think to myself after she's gone. Just ask the Mega-touch.

# Y Knot Lounge

*6331 Washington Street*
*Phone: 303-286-1130  8AM*

*Hipster Scale*

*Dive Bar Rating*

Roscoe likes me. I can tell by the way he stands dutifully next to my bar stool and follows me into the men's room, where he attempts to lap up my piss before it splashes against the back of the urinal (despite my best attempts to balance on one leg and box his face away with the other knee). I don't mind dogs in bars; in fact, I think they're kind of great, especially friendly German shepherds. Beats sitting alone.

I find most folks at the Y Knot Lounge as friendly as Roscoe—even at 10 a.m., when those folks amount to just bartendress Marisol and a seventy-something gentleman in a zip-up sweater and fedora, whose stories about Denver stretch back to the '50s. Talking taverns, he tells me about an era when he and his pals would get off work and seek out bars where "lovely ladies" delivered trays of beer to parked cars. "You could just drink in the parking lot?" I ask, befuddled. "Oh, sure," he responds, "but you had to go inside for the hard stuff." One of his favorite tales, clearly (he tells it twice), involves this very watering hole circa 1980. "This used to be a 3.2 joint, you know," he explains, by which he means it only had a license to serve near-beer and wine. "So kids would buy their booze at the liquor store next door and smoke their dope beneath a great big tree out there." Then they'd come in to use the bathrooms and shoot pool, which vexed the owner plenty. "Wasn't long 'fore he got himself a full license."

A longstanding biker bar, the Y Knot—or Why Not, as it is occasionally listed—hosts roughnecks here and there, but Marisol says it prefers the more respectful, non-territorial Leathernecks—older ex-Marine riders and their families.

The current owner bought the place a few years ago and put in a large back patio with a grill (for Friday cookouts or regulars to self-serve), a tent (for smokers in inclement weather) and horseshoe pits. He also poured sweat and new paint (orange and black, with interspersed Harley Davidson decals) onto the walls. A circus-looking popcorn machine is usually full, and a few modest flatscreen TVs flip between games, sitcoms and music videos.

My storytelling friend drinks $1 mugs of Natural Light; another old-timer who shuffles in after 11 a.m. has water and a couple of aspirin, available in a mammoth-sized Mason jar next to the liquor bottles; I swill $3 Budweiser longnecks before Marisol turns me onto bottles of PBR and shots of Mad Dog 20/20 for $2. I choose Orange Jubilee to accompany my beer; for good measure, she slides me a heavy pour of Blue Raspberry on the house. As Marisol is stocking the full-sized freezer with clean glasses and mugs, a regular named Juan hustles in for a cold Coke poured from the gun. Before I know it, he's got four quarters in the nearest pool table and a look on his face that says, "Well? Are we playing, or what?" I oblige, losing by one ball in the swiftest game of billiards ever played between two strangers. We shake hands, Juan slams the rest of his Coke and then he's gone.

At 12:30 p.m., I finally stumble to the bus stop just outside the bar and board the #7. A Dalmatian in a pink collar occupies the seat directly in front of me. Drunk, hungry, maybe a bit out of my wits, I think:

Why not?

## Random Entertainment

**BJ's Carousel (drag queens)**

**Candlelight Tavern (Bar Olympics)**

**Casa Bonita (cliff divers/gorillas/etc.)**

**Club 404 (stand-up comedy)**

**Squire Lounge (stand-up comedy)**

**Bushwacker's Saloon**

# SOUTH DENVER

# BJ's Carousel

*1380 South Broadway*
*Phone: 303-777-9880*

*Hipster Scale*

*Dive Bar Rating*

"Gentleman's High Class Drinking Saloon" reads a gold plaque behind the sunken bar at BJ's. Where it came from, I couldn't say, but if it was created to refer to this joint, I find it in contempt. Not that Denver's self-ascribed "friendliest gay bar" since 1977 isn't a gem; it is. But it's a dive, friends, right down to the threadbare carpet, puffy green upholstery, ceiling molding and gold stage pole. Other evidence: the carousel figures scattered about, the full-size Colorado Lottery scratch-ticket machine and the incredible mural on the wall overlooking the sand volleyball court out back—which shows 100+ dudes on bleachers kissing, smiling, laughing, sitting on each other's laps and, in a few cases, baring their bear chests. If it weren't so hilariously Wet Hot Gay American Summer, I'd worry that serious volleyball players might get too distracted to play.

Adjacent to the volleyball court, which doubles as a sandy patio when games aren't in session, is the '70s-drapes-and-linen restaurant, serving all-you-can-eat spaghetti (Mondays, $3.50) and famous Sunday brunch ($2.75 Bloodys and screwdrivers), among other fare. Both of these areas, however, take a back seat to the main showroom and lounge, where all the magic happens. Though the BJ's crew playfully refers to its weekend entertainment using the terms "female illusionists" and "female impersonators," the dirt is that, a lot of the time—and especially during random variety shows—we're talking about low-rent drag queens performing mediocre karaoke tunes in the spirit of Joan Collins a la "Dynasty" or, according to my friend Noel, "Tina Turner on crack." The scene isn't always so amateur hour, but even when it is, enjoying the comedy of it all is easy, especially considering that the "dancers" are usually strolling for tips that go right to charity.

During the week, BJ's is brimming with action that is significantly less, well, gay—dart tournaments and leagues, poker, karaoke and Underwear Night, where drinks are a buck off if you come in your skivvies.

Super classy.

# Bonnie Brae Tavern

740 South University Street
Phone: 303-777-2262

Hipster Scale

Dive Bar Rating

For 75 years and spanning three generations, the Dire family has more or less operated the Bonnie Brae Tavern (or Bonnie B's, or Carl's if you've been around long enough) in a vacuum. The near-windowless walls are still teal and white, the vinyl booths still teal and brown and the bar stools still…yep: teal. Though two flatscreen TVs now hang behind the bar, seven other dusty tubes still sit around, off, for no good reason. The coat hangers at the end of every booth remain, and the paper placemats continue to advertise for neighborhood rackets. Once a mom-and-pop affair, today Bonnie Brae is a grandson-and-grandson operation serving many of grandma Sue's original recipes.

On the wall behind the liquor bottles hang oil portraits of family members from decades past. On my first visit, I sat down at the bar to order a drink while waiting for a table and quickly realized I was sitting next to either Michael or Hank, a second-generation son/former owner. His hair was much grayer and he wasn't wearing the same blue button-up, but the bulbous cheeks and Hary Caray glasses hadn't changed. I couldn't possibly designate with any accuracy, but Dire blood ran everywhere—the bartenders (brothers?) bickered loudly with the hostess (sister? Cousin?) about using the waitlist microphone to call parties; their mother or aunt ran piping-hot pizzas to the tables. The energy pulsing through the packed, high-ceiling square room—think three or four generations of family-meets-seven decades of regulars—was lifted straight from a family reunion. My server's name, on the ticket at least, was Mermaid Motor. Dysfunctional? Sure. Comforting? Absolutely.

More restaurant than tavern, the booze selection is nonetheless on point and easy on the money clip—most beers, wells and wines fall below $5. In the early days, according to USA Office of Price Administration certificates hanging on the walls, beer and wine was a measly 11 or 15 cents, with liquor ranging from $.32 (an Old Fashioned or Rye Highball) to $.37 (Scotch). The menu goes on forever —salads, sandwiches, burgers, Mexican, Italian—but the pride and joy is pizza. It's why you come.

# Bushwacker's Saloon

*1967 South Broadway*
*Phone: 303-722-0280  CASH*

*Hipster Scale*

*Dive Bar Rating*

More than 30 years before it was Bushwacker's, the dive nestled among antique furniture stores and bustling Broadway traffic not far from DU was Nathan's, a seriously shady strip club, "homeless haven" and "drive-thru drug store," according to Bob, its current owner. If you left a beer unattended for more than a minute, it'd be gone when you returned; if you needed a fix, you could leave the car running out front and be on your way, dime bag in hand, without anyone but the dealer knowing you'd even stopped by. Next to suppliers and transients, cops were as good as regulars. In fact, when Bob bought the joint seven years ago and kept the name (sans strippers), the crowd remained so rough that the 5-0 finally suggested he ditch the damaged moniker and find a new one.

And so Bushwacker's, the cash-only blues bar and saloon that hosts open mics, jams, and bands on a modest, green-carpeted stage, was born. Part biker hangout, part Wild West, wood-toned retreat, the acoustic guitars, snare drums, trumpets and cow horns hanging from the ceiling can't cover-up what once was. Look closely at the beat-up, red-upholstered rolling chairs, vaguely half-penis-shaped sunken bar and back mirror; then let the recognition wash over you. Add a Playboy-themed pinball machine and beer posters of bikini girls taped to the ceiling of the men's room, and what you're left with is an entirely new business haunted by ghosts of businesses past. Today, Bob is working hard to run a different type of joint – I watch him sternly but fairly scold a group of grown men smoking weed on the back patio—and via solid blues, a smoking-ban exemption (allowed during winter months only) and a Sunday brunch featuring a meal and either a Bloody or a screwdriver for $6, he's succeeding. But goddamn if it isn't hard—the rent's high, the economy sucks and customers are staying home on Sundays now that they can buy liquor. "I'm just barely hanging on, man," he tells me with an eerily empty bar as his backdrop. "But we'll stay open."

## Campus Lounge

*701 South University Boulevard*
Phone: 303-722-9696

*Hipster Scale*

*Dive Bar Rating*

Diary of dive-bar décor: gray carpet, gray booths/barstools, wood paneling and faux-granite tile; empty Patron Silver bottles holding plastic red flowers and six-paned glass lanterns at every outer table; cobweb-covered trophies commemorating multiple sports and strange multicolored scroll-screens displaying specials and scores; a massive hi-def TV flanked by gigantic freshwater tanks filled with gargantuan fish; beer mirrors, sports memorabilia and whiteboards advertising specials in near-illegible handwriting.

Constructed in '46 as the Bel-Aire Café, the Campus Lounge took its current moniker in '49 when the liquor license came around. Four owners later, Jim Wiste—a Canadian who played hockey for DU in the '60s before going pro for a decade—continues to run essentially the same joint he purchased from Jim White in 1976. Like a dozen other dives and eateries in Denver, the Campus boasts the city's best green chile; it's good. So is the rest of the menu, which features Mexican items named after former customers (try Ursie's Sour Cream: Mmm…), a smattering of American sandwiches and fries that, on the right end of a fryer bender, taste like everything else that's been dropped in the oil that day or week. Chips 'n' Hots (salsa) aren't complimentary, but they're worth the singles.

In every season but summer, this is a hockey bar. TVs are in no short supply, but your odds of getting one changed to that other college or pro team you like shrink considerably when the Pioneers or Avs are on. Get lucky and find the actual players all gathered inside for a post-game drink. For the uninterested, a game room through the main bar offers billiards (free Sun-Tues) and foosball tables, Cruis'n World (racing), Big Buck Safari (shooting), Double Up (poker) and Golden Tee.

Scattered about the booths and U-shaped bar, at any given hour, will be blue heads, suits, college kids, hipsters and everyone in between. With two daily happy hours (4-7 p.m. and 10-1 a.m.), $2 shots ("Lots of stuff—just ask"), cheap Coors (though the draft beer selection is weak) during games and bartenders who'll top off your drink at no charge and call you by name on your second visit, the Campus (like the Bonnie Brae Tavern across the street, only open later) is a beacon of relief on the edge of Cherry Creek.

Just beware the "Hot Beer, Lousy Food, Bad Service" sign by the door. And, obviously, the Bar Phone Fees:

$1 – (He's) not here
$2 – On his way out
$3 – Just left
$4 – Haven't seen him all day
$5 – Who?

# Candlelight Tavern

*383 South Pearl Street*
*Phone: 303-778-9530*

*Hipster Scale*        *Dive Bar Rating*

Once a seedy, smoky biker bar where rides (and ride-throughs) were welcome inside, the fifty-year-old Candlelight Tavern now rocks higher-watt light bulbs, stocks higher-shelf booze and attracts a higher-profile clientele—if you can call the swarms of University of Denver kids and alum who flood the two-room neighborhood bar on weekends "higher profile" than bikers. Personally, I try not to judge a barfly by the size of his trust fund, but you get the idea.

Alternately called the Candlefight (partly because of a history that includes door-busting brawls and even deaths) and the Mandlelight (what dive isn't teeming with dudes during the day?), the Candlelight is still plenty rough around the edges, even with a massive flatscreen TV behind the bar, the kind with built-in advertising on the sides. Badly blown speaker boxes pop and hiss with every hip-hop selection on the Internet juke; Air King purifiers collect a scientific amount of dust and debris near the ceiling tiles; the Formica bar top and cabinets conjure discount-bin bowling balls; and the ATM? Imagine a refrigerator-sized version of the IBM 5100 or original Commodore with a 7-Eleven debit-card reader glued to the front. Wicked, um, retro, brah.

Then there's the granular soap in the bathrooms, which I examine in my supple city-boy hands as if gazing upon an endangered species. An ironic throwback? A cheap alternative to bright-pink and orange liquid soap sold by the bucket? More like a holdover from the days when blue-collar hands demanded a little extra grit for all that grease and grime. In any case, it's wonky. As are the very selective kitchen hours, though the six-item menu—two burgers, fries, rings, wings and seasonal chili—more than makes up for that in taste and price.

Darts, billiards, foosball and a shuffleboard table dominate the side room, while wood paneling and trophies dating back more than a decade hold down the decor. The cashews and peanut M&Ms dispensed for a quarter a crank are an added bonus. And the service— Scotty wears a bottle-opener ring, stacks everything served in glasses for easier handling across the bar and keeps credit cards tucked underneath his hat—is efficient, to say nothing of friendly and welcoming.

Tournaments (foosball, darts, rock-paper-scissors) and special events (don't miss the Bar Olympics in October of each year) abound. But if you like it quiet, visit before happy hour ends at 6:30 p.m. on weekdays (well before the door guy shows up to reject fake IDs and enforce fire code), when you can enjoy a $2 PBR and $3 burger in peace.

# Gennaro's Lounge

*2598 South Broadway*
*Phone: 303-722-1044*

*Hipster Scale*

*Dive Bar Rating*

For 58 years, Gennaro's Lounge was a two-room Italian restaurant/ pizzeria and bar owned and operated by Joe Gennaro and his son, Leonard. In late 2008, however, Leonard abruptly sold the building and business, citing health problems and issues with management. Three months later, in February 2009, the Colorado Attorney General indicted seven people on charges of racketeering, gambling and loan-sharking in connection with underground poker games at the Gin Rummy Club, just a few blocks north. Two of those indicted allegedly had financial interest in Gennaro's and used it to launder money from the poker club. Another, a longtime bartendress at the Lounge, was accused of funneling in excess of $200,000 from the Gin Rummy through her personal bank account. Is any of it true? Hell if I know. But the folklore's fun.

For a minute there, everyone was worried that this Denver institution would stay shuttered forever. Then in March of 2009, it reopened under new ownership and management. Thank god. The recipes have changed, but some friends and I stopped in on a stormy Sunday afternoon in May and found everything—the pineapple-and-pepperoni pizza, baked ziti and cheese ravioli—really stinkin' delicious. The ravs took an inexplicable 30 minutes "because the water needed to boil," but the kitchen threw in a free basket of fried cheese sticks as a consolation.

The draft beer has also changed. Though a dated "Budweiser on Tap" sign still hangs above the back door, it's now only available in a bottle—a good thing to know when drafts are two-for-one during happy hour and what you really want is a Bud. We got confused, order Buds and got bottles with no red poker chip designating our second drink free. But when we explained the sign out back to the bartender—who admitted he normally tosses pizza from the kitchen, not drinks from behind the rectangular bar—he took care of us, throwing in our second drink for free and apologizing for the mix-up.

Most everything else seems the same—the red plank walls, white ceiling tiles and black-and-white checkered floor, as well as the laminate wood bar with Susan B. Anthony gold dollars preserved underneath and the ancient push-button cig machine. I can't be sure whether many of the old regulars have returned, but if they haven't, they should see my free cheese sticks and second round for they are:

A sign that at the new Gennaro's, the customer comes first.

# Kentucky Inn

*890 South Pearl Street*
*Phone: 303-778-9600  7AM*

Hipster Scale

Dive Bar Rating

Sometimes you wander into a neighborhood joint and find the stools occupied by a gaggle of sleepy, surly, set-in-their-ways regulars all too ready to give your sudden presence the dreaded stink-eye. "Who the fuck are you?" their silence and stares say, "and what the fuck are you doing in here?" The Kentucky Inn is not one of those joints.

My most enjoyable trip in a series of incredibly pleasant visits involved a nearly three-hour-long conversation with Lorraine, a mulleted mainstay of the surrounding neighborhood and the recently remodeled Kentucky (the owners of the nearby Candlelight Tavern bought it in 2007 and provided a tasteful face lift). Over the course of three or four pitchers of PBR, Lorraine told stories of the Kentucky's well-worn bar and the Denver man who built just about every Formica-surfaced bar in the metro area; of the crass old photo shop owner two doors down who was so possessive of his parking spot in front that he'd call the cops on bar patrons who dared occupy it (this stand off ended when a drunk driver put a four-door through the front of the man's shop and he moved on); of the dives she used to frequent during her underage days—the ones that threw her out for playing "Nights in White Satin" on the jukebox; and of the long brick blocks (blonde on the outside, golden brown from cigarette smoke on the inside) that make up the Kentucky's signature structure.

We also spent a good chunk of time discussing dice and the potential to win a month's rent or more throwing them. Unlike most dives with games of chance, the Kentucky offers customers a renewed chance at winning pots (that have climbed as high as $1,900) with *every drink*. $1 = 1 roll. Yahtzee wins the whole jar, while 4 of a kind or a full house nets a free drink. Pots haven't been as high lately, Lorraine lamented, ever since the house started paying out $25 and $50 for 4 of a kinds when the stash reaches $500 and $1,000, respectively.

So what if there's new decorative brick, shiny wood paneling, gaudy hi-def TVs, brand-spankin' video games and a remodeled bathroom? The carpet's original, and so are the people: The very best joints are remarkable not just for their décor, but (oftentimes more so) for their clientele—the extended family of loyal lushes, drunks, day-timers and swing-shifters who wouldn't dream of letting a little spackle get in between them and their friends. Or their drinks. Or their fortunes.

For damn-near 60 years the Kentucky Inn has been a refuge for the Lorraines of Wash Park (West) and the Drews who wander in for cold beer and conversation. If it doesn't continue for another 60, well, I don't even want to imagine it.

## Best Pickup/Hookup Spots

**Candlelight Tavern**

**Carioca Café (Bar Bar)**

**The Cherry Cricket**

**Don's Club Tavern**

**My Brother's Bar**

**Ogden Street South**

**Park Tavern & Restaurant**

**Sancho's Broken Arrow**

**Stadium Inn**

**Tarantula Billiards**

# Len & Bill's Lounge

*2301 South Broadway*
*Phone: 303-722-6484 8AM CASH*

*Hipster Scale*

*Dive Bar Rating*

As in no other bar within Denver city limits, time inside Len & Bill's has seemingly stopped. And I'm not just saying that because it's a lazy way of describing how run-down everything is. Wander in on an enervated afternoon, cop a lean on the creaky wood bar, watch as John, the daytime tender, hobbles and groans and zones out over the beer tub and lose yourself in 1961, the year Len & Bill's opened.

Dust. Let's talk about it: If it could root, gardens would grow on the ancient television, warped wood booths, pennants and flags and vintage cash register. Disrepair. I'll describe it: The tile and concrete composite floor is one bar fight and a cracked skull away from revealing dirt underneath; the bathrooms are mere closets with flaking green lead paint, rickety doors and a shared sink; and the kitchen, or what used to be? Through swinging, saloon-style doors, a towering clutter of cardboard boxes is spilled over and rotted out to reveal a future estate sale worth absolutely nothing. Just about the only thing that's changed in 50 years is the introduction of an Internet jukebox, which also serves as the only reminder that you're drinking a Natural Light draw or $3 well whiskey in an era when moon travel and the election of a black President actually happened.

But this only helps a little. Because even when the guy saddled up next to me—who rambles about his time in the navy, his deadbeat dad and his ruthless ex-wife even though no one, not even the woman in the neck brace trying to get him to buy her a beer, is listening—borrows a pair of broken eyeglasses from behind the bar so he can break up the silence with a few songs, he plays early Dylan and Chess-era Etta James. He goes back to blathering, John to hobbling and groaning, I to feeling as if time is standing still.

It's 1961 and I'm one with the dust.

# Lincoln's Road House

*1201 South Pearl Street*
Phone: 303-777-3700

Hipster Scale     Dive Bar Rating

For a decade, Lincoln's (before that the Washington Street Exit, and before that Crimson and Gold) has been not just a biker's paradise, but a rowdy-good-time idyll for eaters, drinkers and dancers who fancy themselves a surly atmosphere where bikers and their bitches (riders, not women—though sometimes women) aren't afraid to let loose and get down. On Sunday afternoon, when live music begins at 3 p.m. and the Cajun kitchen—which serves up everything from po' boys, etouffee and fried pickles to meat loaf cheeseburgers and pot roast burritos—has to kick it into fifth just to keep up, it's not uncommon to find close to 200 bikes parked outside.

Inside, even with fancy-new Knob Creek plastic tabletop surfaces and advertisement-embedded flatscreen TVs betraying its more hardcore sensibilities, the Road House is nothing if not legit. Geologists: take note of the petrified wood on the fire place and bar; newbies: have a look at the photographic patron history framed in wood by the bathrooms; tender-hearts: save your pleases and thank-yous, and prepare your superegos for a healthy dose of sassy shit-giving from the staff—most of them riders with names like Sal, Soda and Lance. As I learned late one Sunday night, long after the stage had settled and the speakers had cooled down, if you can take a little teasing from the tenders and regulars, you can expect an arm around your shoulder and a shared shot between new friends. If you can't, well, you can always cry about it on Yelp, if that's what you're into.

When bands are playing and bikes are spilling onto the side streets ("Please respect our neighbors," implores a sign over the front door, "and help Lincoln's by reducing bike noise around here") there's little escape from the madness, though you can try to find it by the pool tables in the back room or on the secluded side patio. Then again, if peace and quiet is your thing, Lincoln's Road House probably won't be.

# Stadium Inn

*1703 East Evans Avenue*
*Phone: 303-733-4031  9AM*

Hipster Scale       Dive Bar Rating

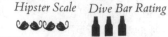

When it opened during the dog days of summer following World War 2, the Stadium Inn—named after the long-defunct football team and its stadium at the University of Denver (DU)—was the first bar in Colorado to desegregate. So says Pete, my early-afternoon bartender. He also says every booth used to have a light next to it that alerted bookies lurking behind a small two-way mirror in the back (still there) of intended bets on horses and sports team. For 30 years, the Stadium—somewhat affectionately called the "Shadium" by the college kids that compose its core weekend clientele—has been in the capable hands of the Saliman family (for a few minutes there it was the Saliman Bar & Grill). Over the years, improvements have been few: new ceiling tiles appeared post-smoking ban, but the teeter-totter tables not safe for standing drinks have simply been moved to less desirable locations. Witness the "ATM table" in the corner by the kitchen. "No one sits there," confirms Pete. Bathroom renovations are currently under negotiation; for now, the walls remain carved to idiosyncratic shreds, the pisser a porcelain trough, the sink hidden behind a nondescript chunk of partition on hinges.

Pete (who's actually the night manager; Carol, the daytime bartender for the past 18 years, is down the bar nursing a cocktail) is full of stories. My favorite involves the father of a former student who called the bar before parents' weekend to make a reservation. For a week straight his son, following a disagreement with roommates, had been charging upwards of $100 a night at the Stadium Inn to dad's credit card under the guise that it was a motel. "Needless to say," Pete says anyway, "dad was upset."

Fun fact: The Stadium sells more Jim Beam per square foot than any other bar in the country. This stat means $2 Beam all day, every day. It also means that the first 50 lushes to sample all seven varieties of Beam each October receive a "Degree of Bourbonology," an honor confirmed the following January by a cap-and-gown ceremony and other shenanigans.

Unless you're enrolled at DU or really want to party like you are, steer clear on weekend nights, when the line to get in wraps around the corner and down the sidewalk. Daytime is a great time to shoot pool or, in the case of the guy who stops in wearing his enormous Mountain Hardwear pack full of dirty laundry, for a quick diversion from reality.

# The Shots-No-Chasers List
*Fewer than 100 words each about some other quality joints.*

## Columbine Steak House & Lounge
*300 Federal Boulevard*
*Phone: 303-936-9110  CASH*

The lounge connected to the 48 year-old Columbine Steak House qualifies as a dive in my mind mostly because it's a lounge connected to a cranky, cheap-ass, counter-service steak house on Federal. And because the Final Lap racecar game stole my quarter, the piece of shit. And because the whole bar smells of meat smoke and A1 sauce. Oh, and because when the bartendress didn't have any clean mugs, she washed a few and filled 'em while the glass was still hot. Which meant the beer was warm. Which is super divey. 'Nuff said.

## Baron's Restaurant & Lounge
*4335 West 38th Avenue*
*Phone: 303-455-4269*

Boisteriously busy one moment, slow and sour the next, when this holdover from the Elitch Gardens days is dead it's depressing as fuck. Especially when, at 8:30 p.m., the bartendress complains aloud, "I can't believe I have to stay open until 2 a.m." It's like, Hello? I'm sitting right here, trying to not hate my life. Shit. If it weren't for the jug of Carlo Rossi behind the bar or the turn-crank pistachio dispenser on top of it, I'd hate this place. But only because it's slow. Recommended: Only if cars are in the parking lot.

## Beer Depot Lounge

*4231 West 38th Avenue*
*Phone: 303-477-0903*

Like an unsuccessful compromise between HIS suburban-basement man lair and HER respectable entertaining space, the recently re-modeled Beer Depot now feels like what happens when a once 3.2 joint dating back to the 1940s tries to reinvent itself on an IKEA budget. Think Target-deco bathrooms, knockoff James Dean glossies, posh silver ceiling fans and a fireplace with a mantle—in a joint that legally allows smoking, still attracts rough-and-tumble types and has a shuffleboard table. Jagermeister is the house wine, PBRs are always $1.50 and the shitty sign still hangs outside. It's all wrong, but oh-so right.

### The Filling Station

*3507 Brighton Boulevard*
*Phone: 303-296-3586*

At this 40 year-old Latino joint along the industrial tire yard that is the beginning of Brighton Boulevard, the neon Bud Light sign in the window says "Abierto" instead of "Open;" the jukebox jams everything from Lost Chicano Oldies to Patsy Cline to Freddy Fender to Bel Biv DeVoe; and the buy-one-get-one happy hour begins at 4:40 p.m. thanks to a bar time that blows in the long run. Hand-painted palm trees, volcanoes, buccaneers and one large Broncos logo cover the walls, and underneath the bar top's laminate rest Globemaster wrenches, small keys, hub cap centers and hood ornaments.

### Lakeview Lounge

*2375 Sheridan Boulevard*
*Phone: 303-238-2149*

Dear Lakeview Lounge: I like that time forgot you—that you have a functional Budweiser Clydesdales carriage globe-light; that your beer swag is, like, 20 years old; that your bathroom is a real water-closet hellhole. I like these things, for real. I like your patio overlooking Sloan's Lake, even though it mostly overlooks five lanes of Sheridan traffic. I like that your bartenders leave the register unattended to go smoke, and that the regulars throw dice and dollar bills at each other. I don't like that hot plates at potlucks ruined your shuffleboard table. Not at all. That's sad.

### Pete's Greek Town Café (Lounge)

*2910 East Colfax Avenue*
*Phone: 303-321-1104*

The lounge behind Pete's Greek Town Café is perfect for nights when you're stuck between the 2900-3100 blocks of Colfax but you can't stand the irony at Rockbar or the prices at Senger's (R.I.P.). Trust me: Bail on your friends, text them that you're pounding $2

PBRs and $5 shots of ouzo and wait while they scurry over to join you. Time your visit just right, and Pete himself will buy a round. The mood's likely to be more subdued than anywhere else within a mile, but the patio's always open (and covered in winter) and the staff is first-rate.

## The Recovery Room
*819 Colorado Boulevard*
*Phone: 303-333-0569*

Like your favorite bar buddy with a drinking problem who jumps on the AA bandwagon and never falls off, the new Recovery Room—which closed in 2008 for tax reasons (or something—allegedly), then reopened in May 2009 with new owners, new paint, new barstools and hi-def TVs—just ain't the same. The parlor games are still imbedded in the booths, the drinks are cheap enough and, at the right moment, the spirit of the old Recovery is still alive. But mostly it feels like a pub that used to party like a dive and just doesn't anymore.

## Ziggies
*4923 West 38th Avenue*
*Phone: 303-455-9930*

I'm not opposed to kids in bars (lord knows that's exactly how I ended up in this position—thanks, mom!). But when it's 10 p.m. on a Saturday night and the stage is going off at a legendary blues joint and there are still small children in the bar? Epic Parenting Fail—one that speaks directly to what Ziggies has become since changing owners, removing all the historic photos, building a patio, hanging fancy metal signs and dropping "Saloon" from its name. Which is a legendary blues joint now tame enough for children at night. So be it.

# Boulder

"The words 'Boulder' and 'dive' will never make sense together," one friend told me. "The phrase 'Boulder's best dive bars' is a serious contradiction," another insisted. "Good luck," was the average, always ironic, response to my simple inquiry: "Does Boulder have any good dives?" The answer, I eventually discovered, is yes. Kind of. Definitely.

# Broker Bar

*555 30th Street*
*Phone: 303-444-3330*

Hipster Scale
🍸🍸🍸

Dive Bar Rating
🍾🍾🍾

A close second to the Outback for Boulder's truest dive, the Broker Bar inside the newly franchised Rodeway Inn & Suites (formerly the Broker Inn) has earned a rep as a worn-out throwback space where CU Housing and Dining Services maintenance crew come to let loose after work. Because it's a hotel bar, it also attracts plenty of transients and lonely travelers content to munch on free appetizers during happy hour and trade stories with the friendly bartending staff.

Part sunroom, sports bar, reception hall and flea-market stall, the mighty room's pride and joy is an octagonal dance floor, above which hangs a recessed wooden ceiling box encased in cracked mirrors, half-burned-out twinkle lights and a disco ball. All around sit fake plants, potted trees, Aunt Edna's dining room furniture and blue-padded booths resting on pieces of plywood for support. Framed CU basketball and Broncos team photos dating back to the '70s line the walls, as does a beautiful floor-to-ceiling mural depicting Denver's Paramount Theatre with Elvis on the marquee. Two sizeable display nooks—one devoted to a rack of football helmets and sports jerseys, the other to potted plants and a tube television resting on a rickety wood table (which inexplicably doubles as the bar's sound system) —let in a healthy amount of natural light for competing on the three pool tables, aging Buck Hunter game and out-of-place flatscreen Golden Tee Live 2009.

The real value of the Broker Bar for the denizens of Boulder is that it's an unnoticed, no-frills, affordable place to grab a drink in relative peace. And in this town, you just can't put a price tag on that.

# Dark Horse

*2922 Baseline Road*
*Phone: 303-442-8162*

*Hipster Scale*    *Dive Bar Rating*

Anywhere outside of Colorado, the Dark Horse would make more sense as a novelty museum or a theme-park restaurant than a divey saloon. But it's precisely because corporate conglomerates would (and probably have) paid hundreds of thousands of dollars to replicate the 40 year-old Horse's antique-cluttered, wooden-surface-carved, Wild-West authenticity—and that much of America would likely be willing to pay a cover to get in—that this cavernous, haunted maze of a place is so absolutely amazing. I seriously wouldn't be surprised if, god-forbid, the Dark Horse ever closes, some developer cuts it into pieces and puts it back together across the country for retirees and their grandchildren to ooh and aah at. But maybe I'm overstating.

First and foremost, the Dark Horse is a good-time roadhouse and honky tonk (sans live country) with three separate bars; a counter-service kitchen specializing in quirky burgers (peanut butter and bacon?) and other grub; an elevated back patio with views of the foothills; and a killer arcade area that features a Pez claw machine, video games and air hockey, among other entertainment. A mess of wooden staircases, winding corridors, nooks, crannies and other attic-like surprises (vintage Mickey Mouse and Friends stained glass? Huzzah!) lead away from the main floor, which may be decorated with more kitsch and crap from days gone by than any other bar ever. We're talking an entire covered carriage hanging from the ceiling, a slew of wagon wheels, full-size carousel horses and the Big Boy statue from the old Azar's. And that's less than one percent of the ornamentation.

A couple things you should know. First: Be sure to have a close look at the bathroom doors before drinking yourself into a 2 a.m. Tums binge or a 5 a.m. walk of shame. Though the door on the left says "Women" and displays a painted woman's leg, notice how the index finger on the painted hand above it points to the door on the right. Likewise, though the right door says "Men," the finger on that door points left. Hmm… Second: If the idea of taking a shot, riding an adult-sized tricycle around in circles (the whole bar, actually) and then chugging a beer—and doing this as fast as you can with a relay partner—sounds like a terrific way to spend a Tuesday night, then Trike Night is your new favorite reason to be hungover on Wednesday.

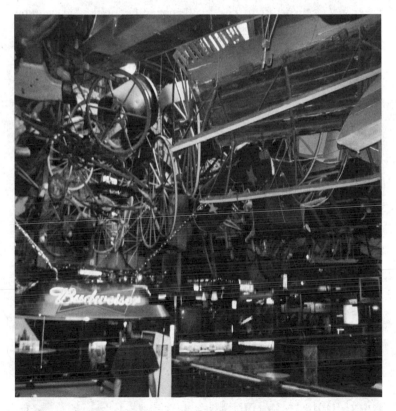

# Outback Saloon

*3141 28th Street*
*Phone: 303-444-0081*

*Hipster Scale*

*Dive Bar Rating*

The Outback Saloon is a by-most-standards massive (9.000 square feet) strip-mall dive hidden from street view and situated behind a Blockbuster movie store. It's also Boulder's only true dive, thanks to its location far from campus and downtown, its 7 a.m. opening time, its mostly working-class regulars and the fact that, at any given moment, you might encounter all of the following characters: an old-timer in a Confederate flag hat, a 300 pound Latino double-palming plastic baskets of free popcorn, a group of suits with their ties on the table, a puking hipster and a pack of 10 college-age hotties screaming and pulling each other's hair. Once, in a span of 10 minutes, I watched a bartendress open a bottle of Southern Comfort with her teeth and hugged a sweet black woman with corn rows named Robby because she heard my friend Molly complaining about a lost phone charger and gave Molly hers. All true.

With nine pool tables, five dart boards, foosball and one of Boulder's only shuffleboard tables—not to mention an impressive American/Mexican menu, a CD jukebox and the occasional live band or open mic night—the 19 year-old Outback is a stellar refuge for grad students and the I-already-graduated-but-for-some-reason-still-live-here set. Younger kids will sometimes drunk-drive or cab out here, but mostly for karaoke on Wednesdays and Saturdays, which the locals and regs take very seriously.

# The Sink

*1165 13th Street*
*Phone: 303-444-7465*

Hipster Scale  Dive Bar Rating

Everything the haters say about the Sink is true: The graffiti-covered ceilings and hanging pipes are claustrophobically low, both dining rooms and the wraparound patio are regularly so packed with CU students that moving and getting drinks are a chore and the food, well, it's okay (though the trademark Sinkburgers have always been solid). But this joint has history. As a building and a restaurant/bar under various names and incarnations, it dates back to the 1920s; the "off-the-wall" flower-power-caricature murals—incredibly colorful parodies of students, celebrities and various other Colorado stereotypes—have steadily expanded, since the 1950s and '60s, to cover every inch of wall space; and Boulder folklore dictates that Robert Redford used to mop floors here. Plus, if you're looking to be schooled, you can pull up a chair to just about any table and read articles from issues of the Daily Camera past.

Updates and expansions over the years have brought an impressive selection of Colorado microbrews to the tap, hi-def TVs with Buzztime touch trivia consoles and an entirely separate dry-goods store full of Sink gear and apparel. But nothing can change the way it feels to wander in mid-day (no crowds), duck down and walk around in the shadow of Colorado's coolest bar art. If you can block out the fact that you're on the Hill—smack dab in the middle of the college-kid rat race—you can almost feel what it was like in the '60s, when you could leave your dog at the door, pop a squat on the jukebox and write on the walls like they weren't so important.

# Rocky Flats Lounge

*11229 Highway 93*
*Phone: 303-499-4242*

BOULDER

Originally constructed as the payroll office for the Rocky Flats Nuclear Weapons Plant, which manufactured plutonium triggers for nuclear bombs, the Rocky Flats Lounge is, in every way but location, a Wisconsin roadside bar: Its year-round Friday Night Fish Fry serves walleye, perch and catfish dinners (slaw/potato/bread) to some 200 hungry diners a week; four types of Leinenkugel's are available by bottle and Red is poured from the tap; and every Sunday during football season, Cheeseheads from across the Front Range crowd the two-room tavern to cheer on the Green Bay Packers. Indeed, the wood-paneled walls exist mainly to worship the legacy of Brett Favre and Packers players of years past, even though one of the current managers roots for the Bears and a bartender wears his Lions jersey all season.

Though its mailing address places the Rocky Flats in Boulder, the regulars know they're really pounding cold ones in unincorporated Jefferson County. "It's a neighborhood bar without a neighborhood," they'll tell you, which means it's in the middle of nowhere, a welcoming destination along the trip between Golden and Boulder. Shift workers haven't blown their paychecks here for more than 20 years, but between the fish fries, Packers games and summer poker runs (bikers are a regular fixture), the joint finds a way to get by.

Six nights a week, a modest menu of burgers, chicken patties and fried cheese are served up for a few bucks from a small kitchen near the bathrooms. While the bartender has his apron on, regulars come around to pour their own drinks and make change for others. The tables in both rooms are covered in vinyl tablecloths; the side patio—half garage, half plywood planking—is a smattering of mismatched furniture and plastic picnic tables; and a white board at the end of the bar ("You bought me what?" it says) keeps track of IOUs and liquid gifts.

Now that the Flats takes credit cards (it's only been a year), make sure you pony up for one of its trademark T-shirts that read, "I Got Nuclear Wasted at Rocky Flats Lounge." Then make good on the motto.

DENVER'S BEST DIVE BARS

*Because Catacombs, Sundown and Walrus are all downtown subterranean semi-dives with door guys, dirt-cheap drinks and density issues after dark—and because no one would fault you for visiting all three consecutively and forgetting which was which—their differences are presented below in abridged, try-to-remember-the-morning-after, form:*

## Catacombs Bar

*2115 13th Street*
*Phone: 303-443-0486*

Befitting its name, this cave of a dive had winding galleries and recessed rooms—one with two red pools tables, another with two green pool tables, a third with black lights and glowing air hockey tables and a fourth for ping pong, dancing and trivia, among other events. The main bar had that bad-ass dairy-cooler thing—where all the bottles were stocked on slanted racks that shifted down when one was removed. You stared at it for an hour, remember? A claw machine by the front door grabbed at gift certificates in bottles, and the landing just inside the door contained a yellow phone that was a direct fucking line to Yellow Cab. Which you also stared at in awe for an hour.

In the basement of the Boulderado, this was the joint threatening to remodel into a half workout facility, half martini bar for the yuppie tourists who could afford the rooms upstairs. But the bartender told you it wasn't happening, at least for a year—that the only changes would be some new paint and slightly higher prices. Which rules and sucks simultaneously. Like Boulder.

## Sundown Saloon

*1136 Pearl Street*
*Phone: 303-449-4987*

The dirty hippies on the Pearl Street Ped Mall who you asked for directions kept calling it the "Scumdowner," remember? It had the license plates and metal beer signs nailed to the floor? The Sue Grafton and Dean Koontz paperback novels on a shelf by the bar? The classic Rock-Ola jukebox stocked with hundreds of hipster albums—The Walkmen, TV on the Radio, Turbonegro, etc.—that was way too loud? Come on: This one had the orange padded booths, the six pool tables, the $1 mystery beer can special on Mondays, the checkerboard tabletops and water coolers with plastic cups labeled "Hangover Preventer."

It also had the separate back entrance into an alley where those kids in hemp necklaces were smoking weed, playing hacky sack, bragging about their trust funds and listening to Michael Franti from the stereo of their Audi A4s. No? Can't place it? Heh. That's because it never happened. But it totally could have.

## Walrus Saloon

*1911 11th Street*
*Phone: 303-443-9902*

This one's easy—the Walrus was the one with huge barrels of peanuts for shoveling and shelling anywhere you goddamn felt like it. You may remember the "CASH ONLY" sign with the cartoon guy flipping the bird, the black leather furniture around the big-screen TV or the side room with the air hockey tables. You commented that it felt like a Lone Star Steakhouse without the meat—and everything else that sucks about Lone Star Steakhouses.

And no: You didn't imagine the two Lazer-Ball skee ball machines. In a bar. That was real, as was your idea to open a joint where the tickets dispensed from a bank of 10 or more skee ball machines are redeemable for booze. Brilliant.

## I-70 Mountain Corridor

"When life gives you traffic, go to the bar." So says a hand-scrawled message on one of the five thousand or so dollar bills lining the walls of Kermitts Roadhouse in Idaho Springs. The next time you find yourself in bumper-to-bumper traffic along the I-70 Mountain Corridor – or simply want to blaze a trail westward for a beer and an experience unlike anything in Denver—instead of hating life so badly that you're tempted to get out and strangle the SUV-load of erratically driving Texans riding your tail, pull off and onto a bar stool. You're home free once you've crossed through the Eisenhower Tunnel and over the Great Divide, so this admittedly incomplete list only includes spots on the Eastern Slope. (A few others not represented here: Ten Day Jack in Idaho Springs (exit 240); Fitz Saloon in Empire (exit 232); and both Grumpy's Roadhouse Inn and the Plume Saloon in Silver Plume (exit 226).)

*In order of appearance along I-70:*

## Morrison Inn

*Exit 259 (or the Morrison Road exit via 470)*
*301 Bear Creek Avenue, Morrison*
*Phone: 303-697-6650*

Though the Tex-Mex is mediocre and the last 25 years have seen the inevitable update or two, the Morrison Inn remains a must-stop before a show at Red Rocks, along an I-70/Highway 74 motorcycle ride or while taking the long way to the Little Bear. The specialty margaritas—the Hog Back, Red Rocks and Juan's Gold—are served in standard (16oz) or suicidal (34oz) sizes, but if you're a mix critic or one to wrinkle your nose at a handful of Sour Patch Kids, a safer selection would be a pint of Coors Light and a shot of agave.

While nothing really rivals the murals at the Sink in Boulder, the wall paintings here—one shows "Juan" leading a train of margarita-drinking, roller-skating senoritas in sunglasses past beach balls and palm trees—are still pretty cutoff-jean-shorts, molestache-tacular. The faded yellow/brown walls are littered with photos of regulars (and the infamous Morrison Easter Bunny); retro beer-vendor shit (seriously, how much for the Coors keytar sign?); and one especially hilarious framed poem (entitled "Clarity") with the added employee commentary, "Left at the bar by an idiot."

If the place is packed (often) or the massive rooftop patio jammed (damn spectacular views), kill some time with a cold one and a few quarters in the game room, which features dropping claws, shoot-em-ups, racing, foosball and a vintage phone booth sans phone. Just promise to leave the cut-offs and roller skates at home.

## Little Bear Saloon

*Exit 252 (or westbound 74 via Morrison)*
*27895 Highway 74, Evergreen*
*Phone: 303-674-9991*

For obvious reasons, the average bar owner would prefer you not be carrying a knife when you visit. The Little Bear—even with its only half-serious dress code of "1. No 'Colors' 2. No Leathers 3. No Cut-Off Jean Jackets"—is likely to make an exception. Why? Certainly not so you brandish it like an asshole and threaten others. Because for more than 35 years, patrons have been carving their names, anniversaries and drunken philosophies on every imaginable surface not already covered by license plates, lift tickets, business cards and photographs.

With counter-service food served in red plastic baskets and draft beer poured into red plastic cups, the Little Bear may not be the best place to impress a date. Unless, of course, your date wants to get Wild West rowdy with 200 tourists, townies and transients while a live band caves in one of Colorado's most intimate stages. If you ask me, any woman not down to shoot whiskey, throw her bra to the balcony or rafters and share sweat with strangers isn't worth asking for a dance.

Housed in a historic building on downtown Evergreen's main street that looks like (and used to be) an old-timey drug store, the Little Bear hosts an eclectic variety of live entertainment six nights a week, opens before noon and continues to be one of the most reputable and unpretentious honky tonks this side of the Mississippi.

## Kermitts Roadhouse

*Exit 244*
*33295 Highway 6, Idaho Springs*
*Phone: 303-567-4113*

Plenty of dives encourage visitors to decorate dollar bills and hang 'em on the wall or from the ceiling. Compared to Kermitts—which boasts somewhere between four and six grand in singles on its surfaces —however, every display you've ever encountered is chump change. Built in 1940 as a gas station and then a bar called the Gold Miner, the 30 year-old Roadhouse is, according to folklore, named for a 7'3" gold miner named Kermitt the Hermit. Today, it's a cult-status biker hangout and après ski destination thanks to a wood-burning stove, famous chili (in addition to other grub) and easy access from the interstate. A former owner used to charge a quarter for directions and put the change in a jar for his daughter's college fund; the current owners still make non-paying customers pony-up 50 cents to use the can.

During the summer, a side patio with a new stage suspended over the creek hosts live music and, often enough for it to be legend, more than $2 million worth of motorcycles will squeeze into the gravel parking lot and down the road. When I last visited, the signature sign had blown off the roof ("Though no one got squished," explained the bartendress with a sigh of relief) and a couple of bored employees had created a crime-scene body outline using masking tape, adding a message on a piece of duct tape: "The last person to mouth off."

## Red Ram Restaurant & Saloon

*Exit 228*
*606 6th Street, Georgetown*
*Phone: 303-569-2300*

Once you get away from Denver and into mining-town mountain country, "dives" are defined less by their run-down décor and more by their history. The Red Ram is a perfect example of this. Housed in the 120 year-old Fish Block Building, this musty yet well-maintained saloon is the real deal, complete with an antique piano (don't touch), a gallery deck with more seating and rickety wooden railings over-looking the rest of the bar and a columned back bar of epic proportions. A mounted, hand-carved ram's head keeps an eye on the action from above the front double doors, photos of Georgetown circa the turn of the last century line the walls and a recently reopened rathskeller holds down longer hours and the televised-sports/billiards scene.

Still, there's no avoiding a dive's signature townies. The last time I pulled off the Highway to Hell for a drink, I spent just shy of an hour with Earl, a lifetime local who took down pints of Budweiser in three effortless gulps and convinced me that my next book should be about Colorado's 100 year-old bars. He then proceeded to list off a dozen of them, complete with names of regulars and bartenders; he also offered to walk me around Georgetown to point out former silver mines and buildings ravaged by fire. I took a rain check on the tour, but not because I wasn't interested. Because Earl's wife showed up to drag his half-drunk ass home.

# Index